SLOW YOUR ROLL

By Greg Graber

Hawkeye Publishers

For more information, please address Hawkeye Publishers
P.O. Box 3098, Camarillo, CA 93011

Author photo by Sean Richardson
Content edited by Cody Worsham

Library of Congress Control Number: 2018945032

Paperback: 978-1-946005-21-2
Hardcover: 978-1-946005-22-9
Ebook: 978-1-946005-23-6

HawkeyePublishers.com

What people are saying...

"Greg Graber has positively transformed the lives of many people with his straightforward, common sense approach to mindfulness. Two thumbs up for his work." — **Jon Gordon**, Wall Street Journal Bestselling author of multiple books, including The Energy Bus

"Greg Graber has been extremely influential in my life by helping me manage my time and stress levels. Because of Greg's mindfulness training, I've been able to find small pockets of time to mentally recharge and maintain focus throughout the day." — **Dave Joerger**, NBA Head Coach (Sacramento Kings, Memphis Grizzlies)

"Greg translates the ancient practice of mindfulness and meditation into a language that people today can understand and implement in the athletic arena. I'm grateful for his contribution to audiences rarely exposed to this important material." — **Timber Hawkeye**, author of Buddhist Boot Camp and Faithfully Religionless

"Greg Graber is ahead of his time with his mindfulness training. Greg has a special innate ability to improve people mentally and help people better themselves with his mindfulness training. He is a major force in the word of mindfulness coaching." — **Josh Pastner**, Head Men's Basketball Coach, Georgia Tech University (2017 ACC Coach of the Year)

"Greg Graber has worked with all of my teams over the years. He has had great success in improving my players' mental toughness and focus with his mindfulness training. You'd be hard pressed to find a better mindfulness coach and mental performance trainer than Greg." — **Will Wade**, Head Coach Men's Basketball, Louisiana State University

"Without a doubt, Greg's mindfulness advice and training helped me to become a *Jeopardy!* Champion. Even under the lights and in front of an audience of millions, I was able to breathe deeply, to think clearly, and to live in the moment. Despite pressure, I was able to achieve a 'flow state' during my games. I particularly found Mr. Graber's mindful mental rehearsal exercises helpful." — **Colby Taylor, Ph.D.**

"As an educator and a parent of a middle school child with a learning disability, I have benefited from Greg's mindfulness sessions. The information I have learned in these sessions has enabled me to be more proactive in monitoring her time with electronics and giving her more opportunities to be creative on her own and live in the moment. As a result, I have seen a difference in her performance in school and ability to focus longer on a single task. Greg's sessions have been an eye opener for me on how to best give our children a good balance in and out of the classroom." — **Julie Cooper**, middle school teacher and parent of middle school student

"Mindfulness seems to be a buzzword these days, but it really should be a way of life. Creating a little space in your day for meditation – even if it's just 15 minutes a day – will improve your life in subtle, but important ways. Working with Greg Graber is one of the best decisions I've made. He demystifies meditation and mindfulness and brings a down to earth approach to his sessions. Utilizing his knowledge and experience in guiding individuals and sports teams, I've discovered that meditation helps to reconnect neural pathways. That's just a cool way of saying that in the midst of calling a game on live TV, I'm calmer, more composed, more focused and have a better retention of facts and figures. Embracing mindfulness has been a tremendous discovery for me." — **Pete Pranica**, Memphis Grizzlies TV Play-By-Play announcer

"Our industry is highly competitive and our sales managers are under a lot of pressure to meet budgets, prepare proposals, coach team members, and deal with customer issues or credit/collection issues with large accounts. The stress gets to be enormous. Greg equipped us with tools and insights to regain our focus and composure when we feel like things are out of our control." — **Rodney Barton**, Regional Sales Manager, Shamrock Foods

"Greg provided our product management team with training for mindfulness in the workplace. His style and approach is perfect for a business environment because he relates well to high performing business teams and leaders. We will definitely be using Greg in the future to help strike a work-life balance and improve emotional intelligence." — **Dana Shefsky**, Director, Digital Product Innovation, Hilton Worldwide

"Greg has been an instrumental part of our program and the success we've been able to create. When you are finding ways to empower yourself it all starts with your mindset and ability to see things in keen focus. When you are competing against the best in the world, operating at your fullest capacity is a necessity. Greg empowers those to be at their best when it matters the most." — **Jamion Christian**, Head Men's Basketball Coach, Siena College (formerly Mount St. Mary's)

"Greg's approach was exactly what I was looking for! Not only did I see improvement in how we dealt with the stress of intense situations during games and training, but also in how each player handled being students and athletes. Mindfulness was one of the best practices I could have ever shared with my team, and I appreciate Greg taking the time to work with us. I am very excited to have him continue to be a part of our team." — **Jodie Smith**, Head Women's Soccer Coach at Alabama State University

"The first time I took the Tennessee bar exam, I was nervous. Although I probably knew the material well enough to pass, that initial anxiety hampered my ability to perform well. Through Greg's lessons in mindfulness, I was able to compartmentalize each question, and I retook the exam. Mindfulness helped me block out distractions and absorb the material while studying. On the day of the exam, mindfulness helped me stay focused on answering the questions to the best of my ability, and not think about outside factors beyond my control, which is what led to my anxiety the first time I took the exam. I'm happy to say that I passed the exam, and I still use mindfulness in practicing law." — **William G.**, Attorney at Law

"Greg has provided my young athletes tools for their toolboxes that are both practical and readily available in times of stress. Given that golf is the slowest of all games, there is so much time to spend inside one's head, and that can be a dangerous place for high achievers. Thanks to Greg, we now have the ability to modify our thoughts and create a situation that allows for optimum performance." — **Blake Smart**, Men's Golf Coach, University of Memphis

This book is dedicated to both of you:

who you currently are, and who you will become.

Contents

Foreword

By Will Wade, LSU Head Basketball Coach

I first met Greg Graber during the second season of my first head coaching job at the University of Tennessee at Chattanooga. One of my graduate assistant coaches, Trey Draper, had been a member of the University of Memphis basketball team, where Greg had served as their mindfulness coach. Trey kept telling me about the great work Greg had done with him and his teammates. He wanted me to bring Greg in to work with our guys at Chattanooga.

Initially I had no interest in meeting Greg or bringing him in to work with our guys. It was nothing personal. I just did not buy into mindfulness or meditation. My limited exposure with mindfulness was when I was an assistant coach at VCU a few years earlier and our head coach, Shaka Smart, talked about how he meditated with some of our players. I thought it was hokey. In retrospect, I had no basis for this opinion. I just didn't know what I didn't know.

Over time, Trey was relentless in bugging me about bringing Greg to Chattanooga. After calling Memphis' coach, Josh Pastner, and getting glowing reviews from him about Greg, I finally relented.

In late October of 2014, Greg was in town because his wife was competing in an Ironman triathlon. With time to kill while she was preparing to compete, Greg came by to talk to me.

We hit if off immediately. During his pitch to work with our team, Greg quelled all of my fears. He presented the information in a no-nonsense, very straightforward approach. One of the reasons his message resonated so well with my players is that he framed the material in such a way that it was interesting and germane to their needs. He was able to successfully convey to them the benefits of mindfulness and how it could help them both on and off the court.

Before he left that initial meeting, I dropped a bomb on him. I told him that he could work with our team, but I would not be able to pay him because our budget was limited, because we were a small Division I team. For some unknown reason, he agreed to work with us anyway! That is the kind of guy he is.

Over the next few months during the season, Greg would make the almost five-hour trip across the state from Memphis to Chattanooga many times to work with us. He would work with the players over the phone as well. Greg was able to teach them better focus and concentration through meditation, deep breathing, and visualization exercises. I also started using his deep breathing exercises to get calm and focused – particularly before games.

Greg had much success working with our team that season – so much, in fact, that I have had Greg work with the teams I have coached since at VCU and LSU. And, you will be glad to know, he started getting paid a few years back!

At LSU, we have incorporated several of his practices in our routines, as they have been beneficial in our performance and overall well-being both on and off the court. The word "BREATHE" is one of our mantras. Our players know the importance of conscious breathing and how it connects the mind and body to enhance our state of flow. Before every game we huddle up and take a few deep breaths together to get grounded into the present moment. This mindset enables us to focus on the importance of playing the game "ONE" play at a time.

As you will discover from reading this book, Greg works with people from all walks of life, not just athletes. He sees it as his life purpose to improve the quality of individuals' lives through his teaching of mindfulness. His approach is straightforward, and he employs common sense and his great sense of humor in his teachings.

Greg goes out of his way to demystify the concept of mindfulness in his sessions. In other words, he dispels the proper knowledge so people can learn what mindfulness is and what it isn't. Because mindfulness has become so mainstream, this helps. He goes out of his way to explain the science behind it without boring you with too much of the technical stuff.

As a college basketball coach, I work and live in an extremely high-stress environment. My livelihood literally depends on the way a rubber leather-coated ball falls. I do not have time to waste on gimmicks or things that do not produce the desired results when it comes to my team. That is why I have stuck with Greg over the years.

Greg has taught me how to better de-stress without losing my edge. His teachings continue to have a positive impact on my players, as well. I am sure the pages within this book will do the same for you, no matter how you make your living. You will enjoy reading it.

I am grateful that you are embarking on this journey with my friend Greg. I have no doubt that it will transform your mindset the same way it has mine.

BREATHE,
Will Wade

Introduction

A late afternoon day in April, 2016:

I park my car in the near-empty parking garage and walk to the side door marked "Players' Entrance." Like always, Paul, the coach's personal assistant, is waiting for me. We make small talk as we take the elevator to the bottom floor of the massive FedExForum arena. When it stops, we get off and walk through a maze of winding hallways. The walls are adorned with huge game-action photos of Memphis Grizzlies players. I always get a rush walking through this area. It's surreal, as I've watched these guys play on television for years. I was a big fan, and now I help their leader work on his mental game.

When we finally reach the coach's office, Paul asks if I need anything. I thank him and tell him I'm fine. I'm left sitting alone, feeling a mixture of excitement and nervousness. I look around and soak in his nicely decorated office, ornate with modern furniture and a big whiteboard filled with diagrammed basketball plays on the wall behind his huge desk. As I wait on Coach to join me, I sit there alone with my thoughts.

I'm an educator by trade, a school principal, but I often spend afternoons, evenings, weekends, and holidays working with people from all walks of life on mental performance training. More specifically, I teach them mindfulness. It's kind of funny that I spend my daytime hours teaching students how to think, and I spend my free time teaching others how not to think – or at least, how not to think too much. From working with all kinds of folks – coaches, top-tier athletes, professional musicians, TV personalities, students, and housewives – I've seen firsthand the benefits of a daily mindfulness practice in just about every domain.

Today, I'm here to work with the coach of the NBA's Memphis Grizzlies. I have gotten to know Coach Dave Joerger well over the past few months through our sessions. He's a good guy, and I really like him. However, he carries a lot of stress, as his team has made the playoffs the past six seasons, and expectations are high for this team to continue producing on a similar level. The pressure on him from the fans, media, and upper management is tremendous. NBA coaches have million dollar contracts, but their job security is often nonexistent. Their success depends on how many games they win, or in this case, whether or not the team makes the playoffs.

Due to circumstances beyond his control, Coach Joerger is not operating under the best of circumstances. His team has been hit by a rash of injuries unseen before. In fact, all of his starters are injured. To make matters worse, even his second-string players are out injured. The team's management and Coach Joerger are forced to shake the bushes overseas and in the minor leagues to field a team. His ragtag roster is the basketball equivalent to the Bad News Bears, so much that the fans have nicknamed them the "Suicide Squad." In fact, this 2015-16 Memphis Grizzlies roster will end up setting an NBA single-season record for the most players used, an astonishing

28! Not the kind of record a coach wants, and not the kind of record that is conducive for making it to the playoffs.

As I wait for Coach to join me, I scribble down a few notes, trying to decide what stress reduction techniques would be useful today. I see it as my job to get him grounded and focused. I'm sure he has all kinds of clutter in his mind from the stress. I'm going to help him realize that he needs to control what he can control and let go of what he can't.

As I sit here, thoughts swirl around in my mind. I think about my passion for teaching mindfulness and how I got into it. I start to smile. It's been an unexpected but rewarding journey.

Years ago, my wife Holly took me to my first meditation class. I had no interest in going. Like many people, I considered it fringe, even strange. As popular ABC News anchor and enthusiastic mindfulness proponent Dan Harris likes to say, "Mindfulness has a PR problem." Case in point: whenever I heard the term "mindfulness," I conjured up thoughts of new age cult members chanting "OMMMMM" at some type of commune while waiting for the mothership to beam them up.

I was ignorant for thinking this. I could not have been more wrong. As with most things, Holly was right. I needed mindfulness. Contrary to popular belief, diving into the mindfulness pool did not make me lose my edge and become some kind of emotionless blob. Instead, it gave me a quiet, calm confidence and focus. Mindfulness continues to teach me how to deal with what life throws at me, instead of senselessly resisting it. I have found that there is great power in learning to focus on what you can change and letting go of what you can't.

After several years of practicing mindfulness, I started taking every course on it I could find from Harvard to the West Coast and everywhere in between. I began presenting on mindfulness at educational conferences and working with groups and individuals all over the world.

Now as I sit in the office waiting for Coach Joerger to join me, I think about how we all need mindfulness. Whether you are an NBA coach who is expected to make the playoffs with an injury depleted roster or the check-out clerk at the grocery store who has to deal with hosts of unpleasant people who are in a hurry, the tips and techniques in this book will help you. Simply stated, mindfulness can teach you how to use your mind, instead of letting your mind use you.

We live in an accelerated culture, where everything comes at us at warp speed. We are digital citizens who have come to expect instant gratification at the push of a button in 140 characters or less. This is our norm. It's difficult for our minds and emotions to process situations and experiences at the breakneck speed our tech-driven-world thrusts us into.

Our minds are barraged with a constant flurry of thoughts. In fact, some scientists say that we have upwards of 70,000 thoughts per day. This averages out to about 49 thoughts per minute. In addition, science tell us that our minds wander 47% of the time. To put that in perspective, you are distracted almost half of the time you are awake!

All that means the ability to slow down our thoughts to get focused and centered in the present moment is a real advantage. In fact, the secret to your success lies in being fully engaged in the present moment without annoying distractions or mental clutter getting you off task. The practice of mindfulness can help you cultivate these mental skills.

I snap out of my thoughts when I hear the office door open. Coach Joerger walks in, smiling as always. I stand up and we shake hands and hug. After exchanging pleasantries, we sit and get down to the business.

This session would end up being my last meeting with Coach Joerger, as he ended up leaving Memphis to become the coach of the Sacramento Kings a few weeks after the end of the season – not before his Grizzlies made the playoffs, though.

Qualifying for the postseason in the tough Western Conference is no easy feat, especially when you consider the injury-laden roster of the Grizzlies that season. Coach Joerger showed incredible mental tenacity in leading his team despite all the obstacles they were facing. While I won't give his mindfulness practice all of the credit for this remarkable achievement, I will give it quite a bit. A less mindful coach would have folded under the pressure.

Coach Joerger's accomplishment with his 2015-16 Memphis Grizzlies team can be a metaphor for any obstacle in life. Using this mindset, we can choose to be crushed by stress or learn to lean into it and make the best of any situation with focus and poise. We can apply these practices with a daily dedication for better living at home, work, school, sports, and play.

As research continues to prove its mental and physical benefits at an astonishing rate, mindfulness has become more mainstream in our culture within the past few years. Many are turned off to mindfulness, because they see celebrities singing the praises of its benefits in just about every medium. Critics want you to believe that this mindfulness revolution is just a fad. The practice of mindfulness, which comes out of the ancient Buddhist tradition, has been around for over 2,000 years, and it's not going away.

This book contains my experiences, thoughts, stories, and teachings on the subject of mindfulness. I am honored to share it with you. Just like the human mind, the contents of this book are all over the place, assembled as a hodgepodge of stories, essays, articles, anecdotes, how-to tips, and metaphorical vignettes. By no means do I consider myself to be a mindfulness purist, nor do I find favor with the trendy "McMindfulness" camp. My path is the middle of that road.

I am an educator, not a scientist or psychologist. Therefore, I focus on teaching, instead of gathering data and conducting research experiments on the subject. My writing tone in this book is intentionally informal, as I want it to sound the same way in which I teach my mindfulness classes in person. I mention a number of books, studies, and resources I have found helpful in my own practice in case you want to dig deeper into some of these concepts. Being a product of my generation, I also make reference to a few songs and movies from the 80's. But fear not, this book is cross-generational in its scope and sequence!

You will notice that numerous times within the pages of this book I refer to the "Buddhist tradition." Please note that I am using this term from the context in which the Buddhists use the concept and techniques of mindfulness as tools for dealing with our minds. I use it in a pragmatic sense, not a religious one. I am not proposing anyone forsake their spiritual beliefs and adopt another faith's dogma. Mindfulness works for people of all faith backgrounds and even for those who subscribe to no belief system whatsoever. The only thing I am trying to convert you to is peace of mind.

Be leery of anyone who claims to be a "mindfulness expert." Because of the very nature of our minds, no one is an expert, myself included. With that said, I do believe that this book has something to offer for everyone. I did not invent the majority of the techniques and concepts within these pages. While I may have framed these teachings in an unorthodox or unique way, I did not create most of them. The vast majority have been around for thousands of years. I do not profess to be a "sage on the stage." Therefore, I encourage you to use what works for you in this book and ignore what doesn't. Use a pen or highlighter and mark this book up. The chapters are intentionally short, divided into what I like to call "bite-sized chunks." This makes them easier to digest.

Chapter One, Focused and Centered, was written by Cody Worsham, originally for Tiger Rag magazine, "The Bible of LSU Sports." It was featured in the 2017-18 Basketball Preview for LSU Basketball. I think this article gives a good overview of how I approach my work. I am grateful to Cody for letting us include it.

As a wise man once said, "The journey of one thousand miles starts with a single step." Whether this is your first step or your one-thousandth mile on your mindfulness journey, I hope you enjoy reading this book as much as I did writing it. While reading, I encourage you to let the yield sign graphic on the front cover and at the beginning of each chapter serve as a reminder for you to "slow your roll," because doing this keeps us mindful during fast times!

Namaste,
Greg

Chapter 1
Focused and Centered

MINDFULNESS COACH GREG GRABER HELPS KEEP LSU CALM AMID THE CHAOS OF COLLEGE HOOPS

By Cody Worsham, Tiger Rag Editor

Greg Graber knows the answer to the question he's about to ask, but he's going to ask it anyway.

He has the attention of the entire LSU basketball locker room, to whom he has just shown a carefully-crafted, thoroughly-edited PowerPoint presentation, featuring LeBron James, Stephen Curry, Michael Jordan and others – all of whom, like Graber, practice meditation, and, all of whom, unlike Graber, are elite basketball players.

Who here, Graber asks, *is better than any of these guys?*

No hands go up, and that's when Graber knows he's cleared the first hurdle in selling a room of basketball players on the benefits of mindfulness and meditation.

Graber, a mental performance trainer with the Memphis Grizzlies and, now, having followed Will Wade from VCU to LSU, knows how hard the sell can be, because at first, he didn't buy it either. An educator by trade, Graber has always been fascinated by the workings of the mind. But more than decade ago, he came away from a meditation course his wife practically dragged him to vowing never to return.

"I thought it was the worst thing in the world, to have to sit there and do 10 minutes of nothing but focus on my breath," Graber says. "I thought it was real New Agey, and back then it was less mainstream. It was very fringe. I thought it was weird."

Given his current role working with athletes, it's fitting Graber's path to mindfulness came via sport. A former high school soccer player at the Montverde Academy – the same school former Tiger Ben Simmons attended in Florida – Graber is an avid runner. He's an avid reader, too, and it was the intersection of those two hobbies that brought him to a more open-minded perspective on meditation.

"A couple years later, I was reading an article in a magazine about the similarities of running and meditation, how you can focus on your breath and how it helps you get calm and centered," he says. "I kind of fell into it that way. As a runner, it really piqued my interest."

Before long, Graber was practicing on his own, attending classes and getting certifications. His headmaster, Stuart McCathie, sent him to Harvard and UCLA to learn how to implement mindfulness training for students and teachers, and Graber brought the practice back to his school, Lausanne Collegiate

School in Memphis, instituting the South's first in-school meditation program. Graber's transition from the classroom to the basketball court came through Josh Pastner, who is now the head coach for Georgia Tech's men's basketball team, down the road from Lausanne at the University of Memphis.

"Josh was always nice enough to come out here and present to my kids at my school," Graber says. "Then he made the mistake of giving me his phone number."

Graber began messaging Pastner about mindfulness training for athletes. He emailed him articles about Phil Jackson's relationship with George Mumford, Jackson's "Zen Master" with the Bulls and Lakers.

"He was a little bit reluctant at first," Graber says. "He didn't know if his guys would buy into it."

They did – with the help of Graber's PowerPoint – and soon he was working with the Tigers on a daily basis. One player, Trey Draper, joined Wade's staff at Chattanooga as a graduate assistant and recommended giving Graber a shot.

"Trey kept telling Will about this," Graber says. "Will called Josh Pastner about it, and then I visited with Will. We clicked."

Before long, Graber was driving the five hours from Memphis to Chattanooga to help Wade's team, free of charge. He's since followed Wade to VCU and, now, LSU, flying in once a month during the season and once every couple of months in the offseason to work with both Wade and his players. He also works with six to eight players individually, meeting with them one-on-one when he's in town and texting them during the season. He ordered purple bracelets with the word "BREATHE" in gold lettering that Wade and the players wear, tactile reminders of their practice.

"Will is one of these guys who is really forward-thinking and progressive," Graber says. "He realizes players getting the mental edge is really going to help. He's willing to try anything, and because he's into it, they buy into it, too."

When he finishes his initial presentation, Graber's first session with any team or individual he works with – in addition to the Grizzlies, he also consults Mount St. Mary's, coached by former VCU assistant Jamion Christian, and has worked with Alabama softball, Memphis golf, and local lawyers and physicians in Memphis – is what he calls "a demystification of mindfulness." He breaks down, from a scientific perspective, what it is and what it isn't.

"I talk to them about the way the mind works," he says. "The flight or fight syndrome, how adrenaline works. How different parts of the brain work and how they can learn to control it through their breath to facilitate focus and calmness."

There are four different exercises Graber leads. First, he teaches how to think about thinking. A thought, he says, is mental activity. It's not an absolute truth, and he shows them how they can observe those thoughts, rather than be consumed by them.

Next, he works on breathing, the vehicle for entering a mindful state. There's proactive breathing – how to breathe before they go into a game, or how to get focused and centered before they take a free throw. Wade, for example, has his own 10-to-15 minute pregame routine. There's also reactive breathing – recognizing a state of agitation after a bad call or an angry coach, and breathing out the adrenaline to restore calm.

Third, he helps them develop a daily meditation habit, and shows them how meditation "helps build the parts of the brain that facilitate focus." Every day, LSU's strength coach Greg Goldin – who meditates twice a day – leads a three-minute pre-practice meditation for the team. Graber also encourages them to develop a routine of individual morning meditation.

"Just like lifting weights is a physical exercise, meditation (focusing on their breath and learning to deal with distraction) is a mental exercise," he says. "It's the mental equivalent of lifting a barbell for their attention span. It makes them more patient, it cultivates their ability to deal with stress in a more responsive manner, instead of being knee-jerk reactive."

The final piece of the puzzle is visualization. It's the "mental rehearsal" tool that players use the night before a game. Graber instructs them to take whatever component of the game they want to work on, and run through a simulation of it in action, tying-in the five senses. A shooting guard, for example, imagines letting it rip from three, feeling the ball leave his fingertips, watching it go in, and hearing it pass through the net.

"When they can do that, for their brain, it's almost the same as doing it physically," he says. "So when they get into the game situation, it's like their brain has seen this and done this before. They are more confident and can get into the flow."

If there was any hesitation among LSU's players, it quickly transformed into enthusiastic endorsement.

"It's been really beneficial for me," says sophomore guard Skylar Mays, who is also a premed student. "With my major and how much we're doing on the court, I think taking a little time away from it, for just five or ten minutes, is really helpful."

Junior guard Brandon Sampson said he immediately latched on to the concept because he'd heard players like James and Curry espousing its benefits. He's become an active proponent, developing a daily practice every morning and every night, in addition to the regular team session.

"If you've had a long day, meditation lets you take everything off your shoulders so you don't bring it onto the court," he says. "The meditation frees up your mind. It's helping my mind be clear so nothing is cluttered up there."

Graber is just as clear on what meditation isn't as what it is. It's not, he says, "some quick fix elixir that facilitates perfection." Nor does it create "emotionless blobs" or monk-like tranquility for the players on the court or Wade on the sideline. Look no further than the broken toe Wade suffered kicking a scorer's table last season at VCU. Instead, Graber says, it's a tool, a net to soften the emotional and psychological blows basketball deals out night after night.

"Instead of getting thrown out of the game, he might break his toe," Graber laughs. "Maybe it's mindful he kicked the table instead of going off on the referee. We look for a growth mindset, not a perfection mindset."

Chapter 2
I Don't Need this &^%$!

"What we achieve inwardly
will change outer reality." –Plutarch

This morning I took a gash out of my face while I was shaving. Sometimes I nick myself like this when I am not paying attention. It happens when I have a million things on my mind and I am not thinking about what I am doing. There is usually some kind of consequence when I slip into this kind of mindless state from time to time. Case in point, I was late to work because I could not get the cut to stop bleeding. In addition, I had to wear a band aid on the side of my face, and many of my work colleagues asked me numerous times during the day, "What happened?" It was annoying.

We have a tendency to get so caught up in our thoughts that we often forget what we are doing as we are doing it! How many times have you walked into a room and had so much on your mind that you forgot the reason you walked into the room? How about all of the times you have called someone on the phone and as soon as that individual answered the call, you forgot the reason you made the call in the first place? Do you ever go into a near-panic that you have lost your smartphone, only to find it in your pocket or in your purse? When driving in your car, do you ever forget where you are going? Are you ever watching a movie or television show and you get so bombarded with thoughts you are lost in the storyline halfway through?

When we operate from a state of mindlessness, these types of things happen often. If you are guilty of this, you are not alone. In today's busy, accelerated culture, it is nearly impossible for our minds to keep up with everything that technology, media, and society in general are throwing at us.

To make things more complicated, our society also tends to put an emphasis on the glorification of busy. We live in a culture where we are always expected to be on the go. Everything must be fast and furious. There is no time to just "be."

When practiced on a daily basis, mindfulness gives us some clarity. It is a practice which helps us clear our minds a bit, and it enables us become more self-aware by learning to be fully engaged each and every present moment. ABC News anchor Dan Harris says it makes him "10 percent happier."

Scientists and researchers debate about the mental, physical, and emotional benefits that can be obtained from having a daily mindfulness practice. When people ask me about this, I implore them to research it on their own. There is plenty of good literature and research out there on the subject. I suggest hitting the internet if you are interested.

When cynics ask me why I practice meditation and mindfulness, I typically tell them, "Because it makes me feel better." It makes me less reactive and more responsive to people, ideas, and situations. I still lose my phone every now and then.

On occasion, like this morning, I still cut my face shaving. However, I do so less often than before since I've developed a mindfulness practice.

Meditation is the anchor for my mindfulness practice. It has taught me to see myself as the observer of my thoughts instead of thinking that I am my thoughts. It has also loosened my ego's grip over me. In essence, it has liberated me from my A.N.T. (Automatic Negative Thinking) default zone.

I still go through the entire realm of human emotions. I am not a zombie. I get anxious, pissed off, jealous, etc. However, mindfulness has taught me how to recognize these emotions and feelings and how to detach from them, instead of hanging on to them and suffering needlessly.

Folks often get into mindfulness for very specific reasons, like to become a better basketball player or to ace the LSAT. Others get into it for more general reasons. Perhaps they want to worry less or to create a bit of headspace in their minds.

You don't need a grand reason to get into mindfulness. We all have a quiet, beautiful place just under the surface of our thoughts. It's wonderful to realize we can all tap into this place anytime we want. This is what mindfulness is all about: finding the peace and silence underneath the clutter. When you meditate, you find pieces of this calm stillness. As your practice grows and becomes consistent, you find longer stretches of inner peace in this wonderful place.

Athletes and artists who sometimes reach peak performance say they are so engaged in what they are doing that they reach a state of flow. Others call this "being in the zone." When we are in flow, our minds and bodies work effortlessly in unison, and we lose track of time. Our senses are heightened, and it feels like we are almost floating. Things get accomplished gracefully and with joy when we are in this state.

Being in flow is the opposite of mindlessness, where everything seems heavy, difficult and laborious. These are two extreme states. The state of flow is on the high end of mindfulness. The state of mindlessness is the opposite of mindfulness.

When you practice mindfulness on a daily basis, you are not going to enter into a state of flow all of the time. You will catch brief glimpses and feelings of flow initially. The beauty of mindfulness is that you know that the state of flow is there, and you can tap into it sometimes. It is also nice to know that mindfulness can help you to be less stressed out at your job. You can learn to be less reactive to that jerk at the office. Mindfulness can help you learn how to breathe and focus before shooting a free throw. Your daily practice can help you relax before taking a test at school. If you are like me, you may be able to locate your car keys more often and cut your face while shaving a lot less.

Very few people who practice mindfulness ever attain a permanent state of nirvana or spiritual enlightenment. Unless you are the Dalai Lama or Thich Nhat Hanh, this is not likely to happen. If you dive deep enough below the surface clutter, you can get beyond the noise in your head from time to time. This is why I practice mindfulness. Stopping the noise is only temporary, but the good news is that we can always return to this state.

One time when I was presenting to a law firm, one of the senior partners, who happened to be the loudest and most vocal in the room, muttered under her breath loud enough for everyone to hear, "I don't need this shit," and abruptly walked out of the board room.

It has been my experience that individuals who typically say something like, "I don't need this shit," actually need it the most. However, I understood where she was coming from, because before my presentation, another senior partner who had arranged my visit, told me that this individual had extreme performance anxiety. Dealing with our own minds can be scary sometimes. It is not easy work.

I returned to work with this particular law firm on numerous occasions, and the lawyer who stormed off in my initial session eventually became one of my best students. She credits her mindfulness practice with giving her the mental tools and emotional intelligence that help make her a better lawyer and courtroom litigator.

Every now and then, I still hear her words echo in my head. "I don't need this shit," I hear my inner-voice saying. However, I use her words in a different context. When she first muttered those words, she was calling mindfulness "shit." In contrast, when I say those words to myself, I am talking about the clutter swirling around in my head. I am calling the noise in my mind "shit." So sometimes when I have had enough, I will mutter to myself, "I don't need this shit," and I will sit down and meditate. The noise goes away…at least for a while.

Chapter 3
Mornings and Daily Rituals

"The quality of your life is in direct relationship to the quality of your habits and rituals." —Stan Jacobs

I hold the firm conviction that the world is divided into two types of classifications: morning people and night owls. Anyone who knows me would be quick to assign me into the night owl camp. Mornings have never been my thing. With that said, over the past few years, I have come to the stark realization that mornings set the rhythm for the rest of the day.

It is important to for us to set aside enough time every morning before we start our day to get our minds right. Our minds are like jet engines. They start ramping up, steadily increasing their noise little by little as soon as we wake up. If we are not careful, before we know it, our minds are flying a million miles a minute all over the place. The rhythm of the day is taken away from us if we do not tend to our minds first thing.

It is vital to tap into some silence and stillness to calm the jet engine before it runs amok and starts flying all over the place. I highly recommend that you meditate every morning. In addition to meditation, there are a few other daily rituals that can help you solidify your mindfulness practice. Reading and thinking about mindfulness is great, but nothing is better than daily practice. Consistency is key. Below is a sample suggestion for a practice schedule. I suggest you experiment with it and incorporate the components which work best for you. Throw out the ones that do not work for you. Have fun with it.

SAMPLE PRACTICE SCHEDULE

MORNING

The morning sets the tone for the rest of the day. Don't be in a hurry in the morning. It is important to give yourself enough time to ease into your day without rushing or a sense of panic that you are going to be late. If need be, start waking up a bit earlier. Do not get out of your bed without starting with a positive thought. Something like, "Today is going to be great," or, "I am grateful for today," is a good way to start. We have 86,400 seconds in a day. Make it your goal to be as mentally present as possible during each one.

When you wake up, go to the restroom and wash your hands and face. Do not turn on any electronics (TV, radio, computer, smartphone, etc.).

Metta
(Loving Kindness Practice)

1. Close your eyes. Sit up straight.

2. Picture yourself in your mind. Recite silently to yourself three times: "May I be happy. May I be well. May I be safe. May I be peaceful and at ease."

3.   Picture someone you love in your mind. Recite silently to yourself three times: "May you be happy. May you be well. May you be safe. May you be peaceful and at ease."

4.   Picture someone who was (or is) a mentor to you. Recite silently to yourself three times: "May you be happy. May you be well. May you be safe. May you be peaceful and at ease."

5.   Picture someone who you consider neutral (don't love or hate them) in your mind. Recite silently to yourself three times: "May you be happy. May you be well. May you be safe. May you be peaceful and at ease."

6.   Picture someone you dislike or consider to be difficult in your mind. Recite silently to yourself three times: "May you be happy. May you be well. May you be safe. May you be peaceful and at ease."

7.   Picture a round globe of the world in your mind. Recite silently to yourself three times: "May all be happy. May all be well. May all be safe. May all be peaceful and at ease."

8.   With your eyes still closed, say the word "namaste" out loud, followed by "The divine in me acknowledges and honors the divine in you." Clasp your hands in prayer in front of your heart and bow your head before opening your eyes.

Meditate

Meditate for 5 to 20 minutes, depending on your experience. *(The next chapter tells us how to meditate. Flip over there for instructions.)*

Pray

If you are spiritually inclined, say some prayers for your mind to be clearer. You can skip this if you are not inclined to pray.

Read

Read perhaps from a book of quotes or scripture. No more than a page or two. Make it something uplifting and meaningful.

This morning ritual takes no more than 25-35 minutes once you get it down. Experiment with it for a week or two. It is yours to personalize.

Shower Meditation

When you get into the shower, don't rush. Clear your mind. Try not to think about your next appointment, task, or morning commute. Keep your mind in the present moment by imagining that you are washing away fear and anxiety in the shower. Feel the water and soap on your skin. See the shower washing negativity down the drain. Rinse, soap, and repeat over and over.

Getting Dressed

Put each of article of clothing on slowly. Think about each piece of clothing as you put it on mindfully. Take time in this process. Give it your full attention.

Coffee or Tea

If you are a morning coffee or tea drinker, this is an outstanding way to breathe some more mindfulness into your morning.

In many Asian cultures, tea rituals are a standard practice of connecting individuals to the here and now.

Thich Nhat Hanh gives us this advice on how we should drink our morning tea (or coffee): "Drink your tea slowly and reverently, as if it is the axis on which the world revolves – slowly, evenly, without rushing towards the future."

MID-MORNING AND AFTERNOON

Breathing

Take deep breaths as needed. *(Chapter Five tells us proper techniques for conscious breathing. Feel free to flip over there for instructions.)*

Consider a brief meditation around 2 or 3 p.m. (I generally do a five minute meditation between appointments during this time period when I can. Some days I do not have the time to do it. Some days I do.)

NIGHT

Gratitude Journal

I keep a gratitude journal on the nightstand next to my bed. After a five to 20-minute meditation, before I go to bed every night, I put the day's date on the page and list five things I am grateful for. Doing this on a nightly basis will change your life for the better. It will fill you with a mindset of gratitude. Before too long, you will start noticing things throughout the day which you are grateful for. Some of the things on your list will be grand, like a job promotion or a magnificent vacation. Other things, like a beautiful sunset or a rainbow, will seem ordinary. However, you will realize over time that very little in life is ordinary. It is all wonderful.

A Warm Bath

Few things beat a hot bath for unwinding at the end of the day. Take your time. Splash the water on yourself. Focus on the physical sensation of the warm water on your skin. One of the symptoms of stress is that it pulls the blood out of your fingers and toes and sends it to your internal organs. With this in mind, submerge your fingers and toes. Use the warm water to open up the blood vessels and get your mind out of its stressful state. Fall into a deepened relaxation state as you settle in. Look forward to your nightly bath time ritual.

Eating

Entire books have been written on the subject of mindful eating. Each meal is an opportunity to practice our mindfulness. When you eat, think about what you are eating and where it came from.

Turn off the television. Put your smartphone away. Eat slowly, with intention. Take your time chewing. Feed your mind while you are feeding your body by taking in the senses: What does your food feel like, smell like, sound like, taste like? Get into the habit of eating in this kind of mindful manner; it will transform your life.

Chapter 4
Meditation

"Meditation is training yourself to see your own inner chaos so it doesn't own you." —Dan Harris

The anchor for any mindfulness practice is meditation. It is important to be consistent with your meditation. In fact, we should strive to meditate every day. Don't beat yourself up if you miss a day every now and then. This defeats the purpose of doing it in the first place.

Meditation is a mental exercise. Much like lifting weights is a physical exercise which will build up your biceps, meditation is a mental exercise that will, over time, build up your mind. It will give you increased focus, stronger emotional intelligence, and a stronger capacity for compassion for yourself and others.

I wish someone had told me when I first started meditating years ago that the objective of meditation is not to block your thoughts. This is impossible! The objective of meditation is to refocus your attention when you catch your mind wandering. When you realize that your mind is all over the place, this in itself *is* the meditation. Knowing this would have made it much easier on me.

There is no such thing as a "good" meditation session or a "bad" meditation session. Our minds have a tendency to always want to judge what we do. Work hard on not being judgmental about your meditation sessions. The little voice in your head, will be very critical at times when meditating, but over time, you will hear it less and less. Just stick with it!

Sitting and meditating will be difficult at first, but eventually, you will begin to look forward to your daily sessions. I think it is best not to get too hung up on technique, so I keep it easy. If you wish, you can focus more on technique after you have practiced for a while.

You do not have to sit on the floor in the lotus position, but you can if you want. I prefer to sit in a chair. I encourage you to try to meditate at the same time every day. This enables your practice to become a routine habit.

I recommend one of these three types of meditation daily. Play with it. Change it up if you want. See what work for you.

Vipassana (Mindfulness) Meditation:

1. Sit in a chair or on the floor.

2. Turn the lights off. No music or electronics.

3. If you are in a chair, have your feet flat on the ground. Sit with your spine straight, in a "dignified" position.

4. Place your hands palms down on your thighs.

5. Make sure your shoulders and jaw are loose, not holding any stress.

6. Turn your timer (or phone timer) on.

7. Tilt your head up slightly and close your eyes.

8. Breathe in through your nose and out though your mouth. (Different teachers will tell you different methods. Do what works for you.)

9. Take three or four deep, forceful breaths to get everything "cleared out."

10. Let your focus fall on your natural breathing rhythm.

11. Focus all of your attention on the way your stomach rises and falls as you inhale and exhale with each breath.

12. When thoughts pop up in your mind, don't get frustrated or try to block them, simply return your attention to your breath and the way your stomach rises and falls with each in and out breath.

13. Continue doing this until your timer goes off.

14. Slowly open your eyes

Faith/Fear Meditation

1. Follow steps 1-9 from the Vipassana meditation.

2. Each time you breathe in, say to yourself the word "Faith," as if you are breathing in faith.

3. Each time you breathe out, say to yourself "Fear," as if you are breathing out your fears.

4. Continue doing this until your timer goes off.

5. Slowly open your eyes.

1-100 Counting Meditation (great for beginners)

1. Follow steps 1-9 from the Vipassana meditation.

2. Each time you breathe in and out, count to yourself.

3. Do this until you reach 100.

4. When you reach 100, start over.

5. Continue doing this until your timer goes off.

6. Slowly open your eyes.

A Few Important Notes about Meditation

When you begin a meditation practice, meditating for five minutes will seem like an eternity. You will likely encounter what is called "monkey mind." This is when your mind is all over the place, like a monkey swinging from branch to branch. This illustrates just how crazy our minds are. You will most likely keep peeking at your timer, wondering why the alarm hasn't sounded yet, thinking it may be broken. This is normal.

With daily practice, however, you will learn to tame your mind. As my friend, the author, Timber Hawkeye likes to say, "Meditation will help you cultivate that important space between impulse and action."

It is also important to be as physically still as possible when meditating. Even if you have an itch, don't scratch it.

There will be days when your mind is more still than other days. Some days monkey mind will take over. However, remember that there is no such thing as a bad meditation session. Even when our minds are all over the place, it gives us an opportunity to see our thought patterns and what is bothering us.

I suggest you find a special place to meditate in your home. You don't need a fancy altar or a whole room to yourself. A corner of a room will do. When you are away from home, you can meditate anywhere: on the subway, in a parked car, in a park, in a bathroom. The possibilities are endless!

See your meditation sessions as a radical form of daily self-care. It is your time. You are giving your mind a rest. Just like physical exercise is good for your body, meditation is good for your mind.

My favorite timer is a smartphone app called Insight Timer. I use the free version. There are also guided meditations on this app. Using this app makes me more consistent with my practice. It tracks your data and how many consecutive days you meditate in a row. Therefore, I am less likely to skip a day. Check it out.

Sometimes individuals ask me about starting with guided or recorded meditations. I think they are wonderful. In fact, I have a few favorites that I personally use from time to time, but I think it is better to start your practice by learning to meditate in silence first.

The types of meditation I mention here are just a few of many. I implore you to explore them on your own. There are innumerable types of meditations taught in a myriad of ways by different teachers. I do not find that one type of meditation is inherently better than another. It is all about fit. Find the type that works best for you. Change it around from time to time to keep it fresh.

And most importantly, have fun with it!

Chapter 5
0.4 Seconds (Breathe to Succeed)

"Feelings come and go like clouds in a windy sky. Conscious breathing is my anchor." — Thich Nhat Hanh

Last spring I had a bit of a health scare. While fortunately it turned out to be nothing serious, my physician referred me to a neurologist to get an MRI. I have heard the term MRI before, but I never really gave much thought to it.

It was a terrible experience.

As I laid on the table, face up, the nurse instructed me to keep my arms down on my sides. She gave me a red rubber ball, a panic button of sorts, to squeeze in case I got claustrophobic. Before moving the huge tube over half of my body, she asked me what type of music I wanted to hear on the headphones she strapped to my head.

"I guess 80's music," I replied.

"Here we go," the nurse cheerfully said, as the contraption started moving over my head. "We are just going to take a few pictures of your brain for about 30 minutes. Enjoy the ride."

I'm not sure why they bothered playing music for me, because it was so loud, I could not hear it at all. The MRI machine rattled, hissed, and coughed like Chitty Chitty Bang Bang. It was disconcerting, to say the least.

Not only did it make a lot of noise, but it also slowly kept inching down in front of me, until it stopped about an inch from my nose. I'm not one to be claustrophobic, but the combination of the noise and the confined space made me panic.

My palms were sweating. My heart was racing, feeling like it was going to beat out of my chest! I was starting to freak out. The thought of having to endure the noise, the shaking, and the feeling of confined helplessness for a half-hour was sending my mind into full blown panic mode.

I had to stop it, so I hit the panic button.

The machine stopped suddenly, coming to a grinding halt.

"Are you ok?" the nurse asked.

"I can't do this," I replied.

"Honey, we have to get this done. Just relax. I'm going to start it back up in a minute."

I laid there on my back, staring at the ceiling, trying to regain my composure. Then I remembered some advice that I often tell individuals I often work with:

Just Breathe.

As I waited for the machine to start back up, I drew in deep breaths through my nose. I held the breaths inside for a second, and then slowly released them back out of my nose. I did this over and over.

Suddenly, my heart rate went down. My blood pressure dropped. I felt more relaxed. As the machine started back up again, I knew I was going to be okay.

I continued breathing in, holding it, then breathing out. Over and over. I did this for the entire 30 minutes. It got me through the MRI experience, just as it has helped many individuals I have worked with in the past deal with stressful situations.

It is amazing something as easy as *just breathing* can take us from a state of panic and stress to a state calm, centered focus. Throughout this book, in subsequent chapters, you will notice that on numerous occasions I will give instructions for different types of breathing techniques for various situations. I do this because in many ways a mindfulness/meditation practice is anchored around our breath.

Our breath is essential to our lives. Breathing is one of the first things we do when we are born, and it is one of the very last things we do before we die. It could be said that our lives could be measured by everything that we experience between the first and last breaths we take. Breath is our constant companion. We can benefit immensely by learning how to use our breath for what it is meant to be: a powerful life force.

Our breath is a barometer to our internal states of mind and emotion. When our breathing is tight and constricted, it means that we are stressed or uptight mentally. When our breath is easy and free-flowing, it most likely means that we are in a good, relaxed state. We take about 22,000 breaths during a 24-hour period. Sadly, most of us put very little thought into this.

Each of these 22,000 breaths is an opportunity to get focused and centered. It's also a chance to de-stress ourselves a bit.

Start getting into the habit of noticing your breathing throughout the course of the day. When you are stressed and your breathing is tight, simply inhale through your nose and then exhale (slower than the inhale) a half-dozen times. It will put you in a better frame of mind mentally by putting some oxygen into your brain.

There are numerous benefits to this type of conscious breathing. When we breathe deeply, slowly, and fully, our bodies relax. When we relax, we allow space for greater absorption of oxygen into our body's cells. More oxygen into our bodies means we have greater energy. In addition this helps to activate our parasympathetic branch of the nervous system, which calms us down, as opposed to the "Fight or Flight" branch which "speeds up" our minds and physical sensations. As a result, our stress hormones and our heart rates are lowered and we can function more rationally.

One of the key reasons that conscious breathing can help us regulate ourselves better is the role of the vagus nerve. The vagus nerve is one of the main emotional highways of our bodies. It plays a critical part in signaling your brain and heart in regulating the fight or flight system. Conscious breathing can hijack the way the vagus nerve works. Breathing slowly and steadily out of our noses (with a longer exhale) does the trick, because this slow type of breathing activates the vagus. Eventually, the vagus activates the parasympathetic branch of the nervous system (the good one!). Once this is activated, calmness ensues.

I have seen the benefits of using the art of breathing in just about every domain: from my episode in the MRI machine, to sports, business, the arts, and beyond.

JeQuan Lewis mastered the art of breathing and used it to his advantage in several high-stress situations. Lewis, a professional basketball player, learned to do this during his college playing days for Virginia Commonwealth University (VCU).

Working with Lewis and his teammates was highly rewarding for me. Their coach at the time, Will Wade, would bring me to Richmond, Virginia once a month to train them in mindfulness. Instituting a culture of mindfulness with them was centered around our mantra, "Breathe." We talked about how to use the breath as a gauge for our emotional states and how to "breathe to succeed."

I would work with the team to stress the importance of conscious breathing on and off the court. The times to "breathe" during a game were highlighted in a manual I gave each player:

> Deep breaths when playing (or right before playing)

> Best to do: before starting or going into a game; before a free-throw; after missing a shot; after making a shot; when coach yells at you; when the ref makes a bad call; when the crowd gets on your nerves; anytime to de-stress; after being fouled hard; before you lose your temper; It helps to control emotions.

> Instructions: Very simple; just take one to three deep breaths. This can be done anytime. Don't worry about technique when playing, JUST BREATHE.

Coach Wade also uses conscious breathing techniques to get focused and settled before games. This excerpt is from an article by Tim Pearrell that appeared in the Richmond Times-Dispatch newspaper on February 23, 2017:

> VCU's basketball players interrupt the quiet in the coaches' dressing room at the Siegel Center on this late December evening. Outside in the

hallway, they're yelling and getting pumped as they prepare to go into the arena to play Howard.

Will Wade pays no attention to the sound.

With no other coaches in the room, he slips on his coat and walks near a sink in the corner.

Standing with his back pressed against the wall, he closes his eyes and starts a breathing routine.

This is the last part of game-day rehearsal for VCU's 34-year-old, popcorn-munching head coach, of reviewing game plans and scouting reports with the team, of stressing details and goals in the quick turnaround of one game to the next, of trying to gauge, two days after Christmas, how focused his players are against a 3-9 team.

While wearing a "Breathe" wristband, Wade clears his mind and tries to calm himself.

Before every game at VCU, Coach Wade would have the players stand in the huddle with their arms draped over one another and take six deep conscious breaths together as a team. The primary purpose of this was to get them centered. However, it also served as a reminder for them to take deep breaths during the game whenever they needed to get focused, centered, or de-stressed. Lewis was one of the best not to forget to breathe during the heat of battle.

For many years, the VCU Rams were arguably the most hated basketball team in the A10 Conference. Other teams' fans disliked them because they were so good, having made the NCAA Tournament for seven consecutive years, including one Cinderella Final Four run. Defeating VCU on one's own home court would make the season for several of the bottom-feeding A10 teams' fans. Nothing gave them more satisfaction than cheering against the Rams when they came to town.

During a five-day stretch in 2017, VCU was behind in two games against St. Bonaventure and George Washington, which did them no favors with opposing fans. In both of these heated road contests, VCU was losing with only 0.4 seconds left.

Cool as a cucumber, Lewis stood at the free throw line, took a deep breath, and then made the shots. VCU won both games.

As the opposing fans stood silent in disbelief after he made the shots both times, the VCU players celebrated and mugged Lewis. A less mindful point guard would have let his nerves get the best of him and not made the free throws.

But not Lewis.

As Lewis told the Richmond media afterward: "I wanted to shoot it. My teammates wanted me to shoot it. I just followed through with my routine, breathing, shaking my arms to keep relaxed. In situations like that, you tend to get tensed up and tight. If your breathing starts changing…"

Using your breathing to your benefit does not have to be anything as dramatic as winning a basketball game with 0.4 seconds left. You can do it anytime that you feel uptight, nervous, or anxious. Use your body's physical sensations to gauge when you need to take some deep breaths. Some signs when some deep breaths may be in order:

1. Restricted, tight breathing

2. Sweaty palms

3. Rapid heart beat

4. "Butterflies" in your stomach

Remember to breathe in through your nose, and it is always important that your exhale lasts longer than your inhale.

I always take deep breaths before I speak in public or have to perform. Try it next time before you have to give a presentation at work or school. Before you go in to ask your boss for a pay raise. Before you have to have a difficult conversation with a loved one. Before you have to read in class. See conscious breathing as your new super power!

I have worked with students who suffer from test-taking anxiety. Often they would know the material, but they would freeze up mentally and end up not doing well on the test. We gave them the following breathing technique for test taking and saw much better results from them when they employed it:

Deep Breathing Technique for Test Taking

1. Before you get the test, take three to five deep breaths. (You do it silently. No one even knows you are doing it.) Inhale and exhale through your nostrils. You want to breathe deeply from your belly, not shallow from your chest. Feel your belly expand and contract when you do it. Focus on this.

2. When you get the test after doing this, you should feel more relaxed and centered. This should really help.

3. Start the test. If you get stuck on a question, either save it for later and come back to it at the end, or take a deep breath and put the best answer. Don't spend a lot of time agonizing (overthinking) on any one question. Again, either come back to it or take a deep breath and put the best answer.

4. Take a couple of deep breaths between each question. This will slow your mind and help you get unstressed and focused.

5. Also, take a deep breath whenever you get stuck.

6. Get in the habit of doing this whenever you take a test, and it will help immensely. Consistency is important for it to work.

This technique helped is a young man named Tommy Kuluz. I met Tommy through my work with the LSU basketball team. Tommy was a senior manager for the team and was also trying to gain admission to law school. He had taken the LSAT once and was scheduled to take it a second time when I introduced him to mindful breathing techniques for test taking.

Tommy credits the technique with helping him improve his performance on the test: "As I sat down to take the LSAT for the second time, I experienced a rush of trivial thoughts. It felt as though my entire life's work hung on the results of this test and the enormity hit me. Using mindful breathing, I was able to focus on the task at hand, which, in hindsight, is the most challenging part of the exam. My score greatly improved, and I was awarded an $80,000 scholarship to LSU Law."

Before every class at the school where I am a principal, we lead our students in what we call a "Mindful Moment." *(We will discuss this more in the "School Daze" chapter)*. One of the more popular exercises we lead our students through during Mindful Moments is a breathing technique we call 5-1-7. I guarantee it will de-stress you and clear your mind. Try it! If you like it, incorporate it into your mindfulness practice. You can do it as many times a day as needed.

5-1-7 Breathing

1. Sit down. Sit up straight. Close your eyes.

2. Breathe in and out of through your nose, not mouth.

3. Breathe from your stomach, not your chest ("big belly breathing").

4. Start by taking a deep breath. Work it from your stomach up to your nose. Inhale for 5 seconds.

5. Hold your breath for 1 second.

6. Exhale slowly, out of your nose for 7 seconds.

7. Do this five to ten times.

Some individuals like to have somewhat of a more kinesthetic approach – a bit of movement – with their conscious breathing. This power breathing method allows that, as you incrementally move your head up and down in sync with your breathing. This may be done several times per day as needed as well.

Power Breaths

1.   Sit up straight and close your eyes. Breathe through your nose (not your mouth).

2.   Tilt your head down a bit. Your chin should be tucked, touching your chest.

3.   Slowly inhale. As you breathe in, slowly move your head up. When you're done inhaling, your head should be in an upward position.

4.   Hold your breath for one second with your head up.

5.   Slowly exhale. As you breathe out, slowly move your head back to the original down position. When you are done exhaling, your head should be the way it was when you started: chin touching your chest.

6.   Do this five to ten times.

We have all been told to count sheep if we can't fall asleep. The problem with counting sheep is that it sometimes makes our minds run! We may try to name the sheep or get worried about the sheep running off. A better way to get to sleep is to count your breath. Try this breathing technique next time you have trouble falling asleep.

Counting Breaths

1.   No music on. Turn off lights.

2.   Take two or three heavy breaths to get started.

3. Breathe normally. Count each inhale and exhale as one breath.

4. Count every breath.

5. As you count, visualize each number in your mind.

6. Once you reach the number ten, start over each time.

How conscious are you of the 22,000 daily breaths you take? I encourage you to make it a goal to use your breathing to your advantage. At the very least, be conscious of the continuous breathing rhythm that exists just under the surface of the steady stream of mental clutter. Pay attention to the rhythm of your breath several times a day; it will give you a reprieve from the obnoxious mental chatter. You will love it. In fact, this will be a place you will want to return to often. Breathe to succeed!

Chapter 6
Visualization

"Visualization works if you work hard. That's the thing. You can't just visualize and go eat a sandwich." — Jim Carrey

Janet is a highly talented violinist. She is classically trained and has spent countless hours practicing and honing her craft throughout her lifetime. Despite being widely regarded as being an extremely gifted musician, she has a difficult time performing in public. This is because she suffers from performance anxiety brought on by her crippling stage fright.

When Janet contacted me to work with her, one of the first things I did after teaching her conscious breathing techniques was to introduce her to the power of visualization.

The way that I approach visualization with people I work with is that I ask them to see it as a mental rehearsal. If we can tap into sensory details (the five senses) deeply enough with intense concentration during these mental rehearsals, our brains think they we are really practicing.

Mental practice like this has been shown to be just as beneficial as physically executing the task. Coaches hate when I say this! So let me be clear on this. Visualization is no substitute for regular, physical practice. However, it can enhance it and take it to the next level. If you tandem visualization with physical practice, you will be able to accomplish anything. There is nothing more formidable as unifying the body and the mind.

I took Janet to a concert hall the day before a performance so she could get a good picture and feel for the place where she would be performing. I asked her to walk around and soak in the details. What did the stage feel like under her feet? What did the spotlight look like in her eyes? What did the theatre smell like? The emphasis was on sensory details.

When Janet got home, I gave her a visualization exercise to work on. I told her to shut her eyes and take a half-dozen deep breaths. After this, I asked her to focus on those sensory details vividly in her mind as she mentally rehearsed her musical piece from start to end.

During her visualization, as she played, she focused on things like: how the violin rested under her chin, what the bow felt like in her hand, what the weight of her feet felt like on the floor, what the audience looked like, the sounds filling the theatre, the glare of the lights, and the smell in the air.

We focus on sensory details like this during visualizations for two reasons:

1. When focusing on these sensory details during mental rehearsals, we trick our brain into thinking we are actually performing the task. Therefore, when we perform the task at a later time, the brain is familiar with the routine and surroundings. It feels like a "been there, done that" mindset. This gives us more confidence when performing the task.

2. When we are actually performing the task, the more detailed we make each unfolding moment through our focus on sensory details, the more it seems as if time "is slowing down" and we have the feeling that we have more control over it. This is because we process the world in three second increments. So the more stimuli and sensory details we can put into our minds during the visualization, the more it seems we are slowing time down when we perform the task. This is a good thing! It establishes a sense of flow.

I asked Janet to rehearse this visualization several times the day and night before the performance. She also did it the morning before the big performance. This helped her get over her stage fright and performance anxiety. She had a wonderful performance, and visualization is now a part of her regular practice routine.

Pete Pranica, a good friend of mine, is the television play-by-play announcer for the NBA's Memphis Grizzlies. I have had the pleasure of working with Pete on mindfulness. Initially, Pete utilized his mindfulness training to enhance his job performance calling NBA games on live TV. As you can imagine, Pete needs to be quick in his thinking and clear with his focus, as the pace of a professional basketball game is often at a breakneck speed. He needs to be able to rattle off names and statistics as soon as plays quickly unfold in front of him.

Pete, an amateur aviator, recently told me that the practice of visualization is a regular part of his pre-flight routine as a pilot:

> Flying an airplane entails taking in visual information and processing that into physical responses that control the speed, altitude, and direction of the airplane. Many of these responses are not innate and have to be learned and then the responses conditioned into our brains.

> Since renting a plane for training is an expensive proposition, many CFIs (Certified Flight Instructors) suggest that their students "chair fly" various scenarios in addition to their in-flight training.

An example: In order to obtain a private pilot's license, a student must demonstrate the ability to recover from a stall. This demonstration requires the student to intentionally stall the airplane, a task that requires several manipulations of the control surfaces as well as the throttle. When the airplane stalls and its nose starts to fall, the student must act quickly to break the stall through a series of precisely executed control inputs.

Working to ingrain these inputs while in the air can be time-consuming and therefore expensive. "Chair flying" students can sit in a chair, envision the control yolk in their hand, the throttle just to the right, and the flap toggle further to the right. After reading and comprehending the appropriate sequence of events, a student can visualize the maneuver and ingrain the proper responses by manipulating imaginary controls. The goal, of course, is to ingrain them on the ground so that the next flight lesson can be completed with greater efficiency.

Another effective way to use visualization is in academic settings. I encourage students who suffer from test anxiety to do the breathing technique for test taking (mentioned in the previous chapter) and then to practice taking the test the night before through visualization. This entails picturing themselves taking the test and answering questions successfully by keying in on the sensory details: What does the pencil feel like in your hand? What does it feel like to sit in the desk? What does the test look like? What does the classroom smell like? I have had a lot of success with this while working with students taking the ACT, SAT, MCAT, GRE, LSAT, and other exams.

Obviously, this is not substitute for studying for the test. You still have to do that! It does, however, give individuals more confidence and less nervous energy when taking these exams.

Arguably, some sports are more mental than others. Golf is exceptionally brutal in this regard. During a typical golf tournament, a golfer may play on a course for about five hours. That is an abundance of time to walk around and "just think."

Visualization helps in this regard. Not only do I encourage golfers I work with to do a visualization the night before a tournament, but also to do one between each hole. It is the same with pitchers in baseball who I work with. I encourage them to do their mental rehearsal the night before the game and in between innings in the dugout.

Here are some general instructions for visualization I have given college and professional basketball players I have worked with over the years:

1.   Pick a task you want to improve, such as free throw shooting, your three-point shot, locking someone down on defense, etc.

2.   Sit on a chair with your feet on the ground. Your back should be straight. Eyes closed. Lights off. No music.

3.   Picture yourself in your home gym.

4. Try to use all of your senses: What does it look like? What does it sound like? What does it smell like? What does it feel like (the ball and your feet on the court, etc.)?

5. Practice successfully completing the task ten times in a row, using all of the details above each time.

6. It will become a habit.

When I work with basketball teams, we tailor the visualization to suit the player's position. For instance, point guards may opt to visualize bringing the ball down the court. A shooting guard may customize his visualization routine to be centered on taking three-pointers. A big post player, like a power forward or center, may focus their visualizations on driving to the basket or rebounding.

You can take the basic instructions above and tweak them to make visualizations for yourself. You can improve any task or skill by doing this. Pair up your visualization exercise with actual practice in any endeavor, and you will be unstoppable.

What is something you would like to do better? It can be work-related. Perhaps you want to get better at giving PowerPoint presentations to your team. Or maybe you want to feel more confident speaking to potential clients as a real estate agent. Maybe you want to feel less stress as a check-out cashier. The possibilities for improved work performance through the practice of visualization are endless. Get creative with it.

Another way to use visualization is to practice a task or performance going wrong, but you manage to get out of the jam. For example, as we discuss in Chapter 9, I have worked with Ironman triathletes who compete in crazy races that push them to go beyond the limits of endurance by swimming 2.4 miles, biking 112 miles, and then running a marathon (26.2 miles) – all of which must be completed in under 17 hours. When a competitor is racing these kinds of distances for that long amount of time, it is safe to assume that not everything will go as planned. Therefore, I have them mentally rehearse "getting out of jams."

Some of the jams I have Ironmen getting out of may include: overcoming getting kicked in the head by a fellow swimmer during the open-water swim, successfully fixing a flat tire on the bike course, or overcoming a cramp or stomach problems on the marathon run. By picturing these possible (sometimes probable) scenarios, they are not surprised when they happen. By envisioning themselves successfully triumphing over these obstacles, they are equipped to deal with them mentally. If they practice properly, they feel almost invincible come race time.

You can work with this type of "getting out of a jam" visualization in almost any sport or activity. Baseball pitchers can mentally rehearse getting themselves out of a full count with the bases loaded. Golfers can mentally work on overcoming bad shots to salvage a tournament day. Basketball players can work on visualizing being down by one point with five seconds left on an inbounds pass play. The possibilities are infinite.

Putting your plan into action by teaming our practice and physical efforts with visualization can be a real difference-maker in our lives. As author Robert Collier wisely opined, "Visualize this thing that you want, see it, feel it, believe in it. Make your mental blueprint, and begin to build."

Chapter 7
And They Called Him the Streak

"One person's dedication is another's obsession." — Anonymous

Sometimes when I tell people I'm a streaker, I get funny looks. I think they imagine I am one of those infamous streakers from the 1970s who ran naked through public places. This strange fad was popular for a short while. Streakers would run naked in packs, usually as a prank, a dare, for publicity, or to protest something. Streaking became so popular that country singer Ray Stevens had a hit on the pop charts called "The Streak." (If you are too young to know anything about this phenomenon of bygone days, look up the song. It's pretty funny.)

Rest assured, this is not the type of streaking I am involved with. Let me explain.

Several years back, I was working with Coach Wade when he was the head basketball coach at the University of Tennessee-Chattanooga. We were trying to build mental toughness for his players. As a result, I came up with the idea to put each of his players on a "365-day streak challenge." We were under the impression that if these players would commit to doing one task every single day for 365 days in a row, it would make them more mentally tough. In addition, it would cultivate a positive habit and make them better for doing it.

So, on New Year's Day 2015, we gave them the challenge to do something constructive once a day for the entire year. Tasks were as simple as keeping a daily journal, calling their parents, meditating, posting a motivational quote or reading Scripture. The only stipulations were that the task had to be positive, and it could not be basketball related.

The players were told to keep a calendar on their walls and check off each day they successfully completed the task. Coach Wade would text the players to check on their progress every Sunday.

A few days before January 1st when the project was about to begin, I received a phone call from Coach Wade. He wanted to know if I "practiced what I preached" by asking me what task I was going to commit to for this challenge.

"I have already started," I told him. "I started my run streak on Thanksgiving."

I explained to him that I had started a holiday run streak challenge that I read about in *Runner's World* magazine that entailed running every day, at least a one mile minimum, from Thanksgiving to New Year's Day.

My initial intention with the holiday run streak was just to get in shape for the holidays. However, I enjoyed running every day so much that I decided to try to run as many years as I could without breaking the daily streak. On some days I would run three or four miles. A couple of times per week on "rest days" I would only run the minimum one mile. On occasion, for fun, I would race a 5K or a half-marathon.

Doing this every day served several purposes. It kept me in outstanding shape. There was also a mental component to it. Running like this was a great outlet for stress, but it also made me more mentally tough. There were many days when I did not want to run, but I made myself. I always felt better for doing it.

When I told Coach Wade about my run streak, he decided that he would start his own run streak. In fact, he started his run streak on January 1, 2015, when his players at Chattanooga started their 365-day challenge.

Almost a year after we started our respective run streaks, the *New York Times* did a story on it. By that time Coach Wade had left Chattanooga to return to VCU as their head coach. The headline to Zach Schonbrun's article was *"Virginia Commonwealth Coach Leads by Example, One Mile at a Time."*

Coach Wade told Schonbrun, "I ask my team to be disciplined. I've got to be disciplined as well." Not only was Coach Wade improving his own life with his streak, but he was influencing many others as well, including his players. His streak was serving as a wonderful example of self-discipline, dedication, and mental toughness. We received so much publicity from this article that Coach Wade started getting asked about it from media members, fans, and referees on a frequent basis!

We even had friends who were coaches at other universities who started their own run streaks, including Jamion Christian, then the basketball coach at Mount St. Mary's (now at Siena College), and Jodie Smith, the women's soccer coach at Alabama State University.

Some people thought we were nuts for doing this. Others seemed to understand. As I told Schonbrun in his article, "One person's dedication can seem like an obsession to another."

Coach Wade enjoyed the physical benefits of his run streak, but his main reason for doing it was for what it did for his mental game. As he told Schonbrun, "It clears my mind and allows me to plan my day, all those sorts of things," Wade said. "It's just my way of making sure I'm in shape, more mentally sharp. It's just become a routine for me."

After time, I saw this run streak as part of my mindfulness and meditation practice. I wrote this journal entry on the day I reached my 365th day:

> I have run 365 consecutive days. I have run at least one mile or more (usually more) on these days. This run streak, which started on November 27th, 2014, Thanksgiving Day, has taught me a lot about people, places, and things. Doing anything productive for 365 days is not easy. During this run streak, I've learned more about life running every day than I have in any graduate school course I have ever taken. It has taught me a lot about myself, primarily that there is always room for more self-discipline and

that one person's apparent obsession is another person's dedication.

I have run in the rain, in snow, and on ice. I have run in one hundred degree temperatures. I have run in California and Boston and many places in between – but mostly in Memphis. I have run on the roads, on trails, on the beach, and even a time or two on treadmills. I have run early in the morning as the sun was rising, and I have run late at night long after it has set for the day. I have run on an empty belly, and I have run after big feasts. I have run a time or two after having too many beers. I have run on non-eventful days, and I have run on every holiday. I have run in some races, and I have run just for fun.

There were days when my body felt strong and the runs were easy. There were days when my body hurt like hell and I could barely slog through a mile. There were days I wanted to give it all up and quit the streak. There were days when I thought I could maintain the streak for several years. There were days when I was fast, and there were days when I was slow.

Sometimes I will run with other people, but I usually like to run alone. Some people wave and say hello when I run past them. Some ignore me. Some really nice ones offer kind words of encouragement. People who seem to lack self-discipline are often turned off by my run streak, while individuals who are highly driven are often inspired by it. Coach Pastner of the Tigers and Coach Joerger of the Grizzlies sometimes ask me how my streak is going. Coach Wade of VCU was so fired up about it, he started his own run streak. I also convinced my friend Rick to start a run streak. My wife, Holly, has been doing a great job with her streak as well, and friends like Rick, Houston, Steve, and Randy continue to inspire me with their daily runs.

Running is a part of my daily meditation practice. It gets me focused and centered, and it also makes me feel one with the universe, because it puts things into sync. I don't listen to music when I run. I focus on my breathing and my form. The rhythmic sound of my feet hitting the ground sometimes clears my mind. Other times it helps me to generate creative ideas.

This streak has helped to define who I am to others and to myself. Running every day has also made me realize that this is one of the main ways I experience life. It helps me process ideas, thoughts, emotions, and feelings. A day will come when I will not be able to run every day. I realize this. I am just grateful that today is not that day. Happy Thanksgiving.

Sadly that day came on June 6, 2017. On this day, my run streak ended after 922 days due to multiple knee injuries (which were not running related). I felt sad that I did not quite make three years on my streak, but I am happy for the experiences the streak gave me. My journal entry on that day:

> I had not put a lot of thought into quitting. However, when I woke up today, I knew I would not run. At 922 days, my run streak is over. After learning to listen to my body through running and meditation, I was ready to end it. My knees and my left foot told me to stop. You learn a lot from running for 922 consecutive days. You learn a lot about yourself, and you learn a lot about life in general. The outpouring of love and support from friends has been tremendous. I am grateful. I plan to start thinking about the next adventure while my body heals.

I am also happy to say that as I write this, Coach Wade is still on his streak (around day 1,300). Now the coach at LSU, this streak has sustained him through three coaching jobs. He can often be seen running down by the lake around campus. Jamion Christian and Jodie Smith are still going strong as well, both around the two year mark.

The experience of my run streak made me realize the importance of daily rituals and habit. Habits and rituals define who we are. Cultivating them can make us stronger, more self-aware, and dedicated to the things which are important to us. In some regards, our daily habits and rituals can help align our actions with our values. With this in mind, I came to realize that my run streak transformed me in ways that were much bigger in scope than just the physical act of running. It gave me a different way of looking at life and myself. In an ever-changing world, it gave me a daily anchor. It also gave me a vehicle in which to experience the world around me.

Having developed an awareness about the importance of daily rituals, shortly after my run streak ended, I decided to give more attention to another streak I had started, my meditation streak. Meditation is nothing new to me. For the most part, I have meditated consistently on a daily basis. However, from time to time, I would miss a day or two. Sometimes the day or two would turn into three or four days. I feel better when I meditate, so I set a goal of not missing any more days.

A friend told me about the Insight Meditation app (*mentioned in Chapter 4*). One of the cool features on this app is that it logs your daily meditation sessions. It keeps track of how many consecutive days I meditate. My current meditation streak started on March 27, 2017. I am still going strong!

I realize that I will miss a day meditating at some point. It's inevitable. It may be because I am traveling on the road, or sick, or for some other unforeseen reason. The point of these streaks is not perfection. The point of these streaks is growth from challenging yourself to do something on a daily basis. I will be disappointed when my meditation streak ends, but I will start another one. I may also start another kind of streak.

Think about a daily ritual, activity, or habit you would like to cultivate. Make it something positive that will improve the quality of your life. It should be something meaningful to you. You don't have to run every day. Maybe you could start something like a "random act of kindness" daily streak or a walking streak, or an "I'm going to tell my loved ones how much I care about them" daily streak.

The possibilities are endless. Everyone wins when you do something you love that is positive every day. The people around you will notice a difference in you, as you will be in a good mood from your daily sense of accomplishment. In the process, you will build your self-discipline.

When Coach Wade was asked about what his players thought of his run streak he said, "They all think I'm crazy." So at the very least, starting your own streak, no matter what it is, will give the people around you something to talk about.

My good friend and colleague, Josh Savage, and his wife Niki Savage, have a different type of streak they started a few years back. Instead of performing a task every day for a year, they sacrifice one thing every month. Their "giving up one thing we don't need a month streak," was originally inspired by the Christian holiday of Lent. Josh and Niki realized that that they could improve their lives mentally, physically, and spiritually by giving up something that they did not need. In addition, they saw this type of streak as an opportunity to build up their mental toughness in the process.

Josh explains: "A few of things we have given up for a month in the past are: social media, coffee, meat, pizza. Basically, it gives us an opportunity to be more in tune with how our bodies and minds feel with or without these things. Is it helpful? Do we feel better or healthier? No effect? After the month is over we can reassess. For example, we eat less meat now, and we give up email and social media at least one day a week."

Josh writes that one of the things he gave up that made the most difference in his life was clutter:

> Last November, my goal was to get rid of something I own every day of the month.
>
> The first week or two were really easy. I basically cleaned out unwanted items like old ties, shirts, and other clothes that I didn't wear anymore. Then I went around the house and cleaned out the kitchen cabinets, the utility room, pretty much every area of the house. My home was getting cleaned, but I didn't feel like I was meeting my true goal.
>
> What I really wanted was to part with the stuff that might hold sentimental value, but was actually useless and had been collecting dust for years. I have never been a pack rat, per se, but I have always been the one in the family to inherit the antique furniture, the coin collections, and so on. Basically, I have too much shit!
>
> By the end of the month, I gave away or sold way more than an item a day. It still felt like I had too much stuff and so I planned on doing it again soon.
>
> Decluttering is good for physical (and digital) space, but it's also good for the mental space. I feel less anxious and am able to focus more. I know where things are and don't waste time

looking for them (well, not as often, anyway). Now if I can make the shift towards my future purchases and just not bring as much home in the first place.

What are a few things that you could give up temporarily that do not serve you well? It may be worth trying out. Go on a mini month-long streak to test it. Like Josh and Niki, you may end up building some positive and healthy permanent habits in the process.

Chapter 8
Rewire Your Brain

"The surface of the earth is soft and impressible by the feet of men; and so with the paths which the mind travels. How worn and dusty, then, must be the highways of the world, how deep the ruts of tradition and conformity!" —Thoreau

One of my favorite coaches to work with is Josh Pastner. Josh, who is now the basketball coach at Georgia Tech, gave me my break doing mindfulness training with sports teams when he was the coach at the University of Memphis. I had the pleasure of working with him and his players every day for three seasons.

Over the years, Josh and I have become good friends. And of his many positive qualities, I admire and most deeply respect the way he deals with anger.

My hometown of Memphis is a basketball city. The passion we have for the University of Memphis Tigers and our NBA franchise, the Grizzlies, is often fanatical. We take a lot of pride in the long, successful history of our Tigers. Even though they have never won a national championship, they have been to three Final Fours and are expected to make the NCAA Tournament every year. Expectations are a bit high, to say the least. It would be fair to say that when it comes to the subject of the Memphis Tigers, our fans and media are over the top. In some ways this makes sense, since "fan" is short for "fanatic."

When legendary coach John Calipari left the Memphis Tigers to take the job at Kentucky, no one wanted to fill his shoes. Despite being considered a good coaching job, seemingly no one wanted it. It was turned down by many, until Pastner, who was the third assistant on Calipari's squad, took it. The fans and media expected a big name hire. Instead, they got a neophyte.

Because Pastner was 31 years old and had no head coaching experience, no one thought that he would make it longer than one or two years. It was common speculation that he was the transition guy – basically, he would fill in for a season or two until another big name coach could be hired.

To his credit, Pastner did a good job making it seven seasons; much longer than anyone expected. He led the team to four consecutive NCAA tournaments, and ended up with close to a 70 percent winning percentage over those seven years. Most fans around the nation would be happy if their team had that kind of record, but not the people in my beloved city.

Pastner was crucified by fans and the local media on a daily basis. For thre years, critics around the city publicly called for him to be fired; it was unfair and terrible. The animus spewed on social media towards him was massive and unrelenting. It was so bad near the end of his tenure that the lead pastor from one of the city's largest and most popular churches tweeted he was praying to God that Pastner be fired.

While Pastner was never happy about the way many of the fans and media treated him in Memphis, he never appeared to get angry about it. I was always amazed at how he handled it. He showed a great amount of class and emotional intelligence. A year after he left Memphis for Georgia Tech, a reporter from the Atlanta Journal Constitution asked him if he had any ill will towards Memphis. His response: "I don't believe in ill will or playing the 'I told you so' game, and secondly, man, I really try to stay out of holding onto resentment or anger. The person who holds on, the one that is angry or has resentment, it's like holding a hot piece of coal. You're the one who gets burned."

By using the quote as a basis for his response to someone's anger every time, he was rewiring his brain in a positive way. Over time, this became his default thinking mode. Neurologists claim that every time someone resists acting on anger, they are rewiring their brain to be more calm and loving.

There is a popular saying in the world of mindfulness: "Neurons that fire together wire together." This one sentence pretty much encapsulates the concept of neuroplasticity.

Neuroplasticity is the change of neural pathways and synapses caused by our behaviors, experiences, and environment. When these changes occur, the brain goes through a "synaptic pruning," in which it deletes neural connections that are no longer needed (due to lack of use). After the "pruning," the ones deemed more useful are strengthened. Simply put, what we don't use is pruned out, and what we do use is strengthened.

Sometimes when working with individuals I will encourage them to "rewire their brains." When I say this to them, they often look at me like I am crazy, as if I am telling them to perform a lobotomy on themselves with a butter knife!

Until a few decades ago, science told us that our nervous system was fixed and non-regenerative. However, due to numerous breakthrough studies in the last two decades, it is now commonly accepted that by learning to control the way we approach our thoughts we can reshape our neuropathways and rewire our brains to our benefit.

So, in essence, neurons that fire together do indeed wire together. This means our thoughts can physically reshape our brains. We can cut neuropathways to more positive, productive, and beneficial ways of thinking, responding, and interacting.

Research has shown how thinking, experience, and practice can strengthen our brains in positive ways. For example, before being licensed, London cab drivers are put through grueling extensive training where they are required to learn all of the streets and routes through their entire large city. Upon examination, it was discovered that these cabbies had thickened neural layers in their hippocampus region of the brain. This is the part of the brain responsible for memories and learning. Just like lifting weights builds up your biceps, the mental exercise of learning the cab routes built up this part of their brains and generated new tissue.

Meditation also builds up the brain. Neuroscientist Sara Lazar has done quite a bit of research in this area. I have had the honor to see her present several times at Harvard. She has conducted experiments and studied brain scans of meditators for years and has come to the conclusion that meditation can actually change the structure of the brain.

MRI scans show that long-time meditators had thicker gray matter in the prefrontal cortex of the brain, which is responsible for working memory and executive functioning. She also discovered that meditators had increased gray matter in the hippocampus. Another interesting discovery from Lazar's studies is that meditators had less gray matter in the amygdala part of the brain. The amygdala is the fight or flight part of the brain which is over fear and anxiety. Having less gray matter there is a positive. This makes us more responsive and less reactive during stressful situations.

In addition to meditation and practice, there are many ways to rewire your brain. Here are a few I suggest:

1. When the mind is left to its own devices, it will repeat the same old tired stories. Most of the time this is not helpful, as these stories are fear-based and self-defeating. Choose a thought (or story) of your own. Something that is helpful and positive. Make an effort to repeat it over and over to yourself thought out the day, every day. Make it a practice. If you do this

enough, this loop will become your default thought setting. It will become automatic. This will transform your life.

2.   Control your media intake (not too much negative news, drama, stressful stories).

3.   Get into the habit of using positive self-talk.

4.   Practice gratitude (be thankful for what you have, not what you don't have).

5.   Treat yourself and others with compassion.

6.   Realize most of the time that anger is a fear-based emotion. Let it go.

7.   Try to bring meaningfulness to every moment, no matter how small that moment may seem.

8.   Don't expect every minute of your life to be stress-free. Face obstacles as if they are opportunities for learning and personal growth.

9.   Get into the habit of smiling whenever you can.

10.   Wake up in a positive way (meditation, prayer, reading scripture or inspirational quotes).

11.   Go to bed on a good note (meditation, prayer, journaling, or reading something uplifting).

Every time you choose to be in the present moment instead of picking up your smartphone, you are rewiring your brain. Every time you choose to not react impulsively to someone who has treated you rudely, you are rewiring your brain. Every time you choose not to be judgmental, you are rewiring your brain. Every time you choose not to flip someone the finger when they cut you off in traffic, you are rewiring your brain. Every time you choose not to feel bad about yourself when someone insults you, you are rewiring your brain. Every time you choose to be grateful for all you have instead of worrying about what you don't have, you are rewiring your brain.

Do you see how this works? What are some other ways you can practice this? The possibilities are endless. Get started working on rewiring your brain today.

Chapter 9
The Nature of Suffering

"Out of suffering have emerged the strongest souls; the most massive characters are seared with scars." —Kahlil Gibran

I'm waiting for Holly at the bike transition pit. The Ironman Tracker app on my smartphone estimates that she should have already been in about ten minutes ago. She's been on the bike course for seven and a half hours. The winds are blowing hard and the rain is cold, not exactly the best conditions for riding 112 miles on a bicycle with 2,500 other racers. I always worry about her when she's out there, but today is worse. It's difficult to stand by helplessly while someone you love is suffering.

I am here to support Holly, as she is racing in Ironman Louisville. This is the fifth Ironman triathlon she has competed in. Ironman is widely recognized as the world's toughest endurance competition, requiring its participants to swim 2.4 miles in open water, then jump on a bike course for 112 miles, and finish it off by running a marathon: 26.2 miles. There is usually a time limit in which the three events must be completed in typically 16 or 17 hours. Racers spend thousands of hours training for these races, quite often years, and there is no guarantee they will make it. In fact, many do not make the cut-off time in these races.

Needless to say, an Ironman race pushes its participants to their physical, mental, and emotional limits. It's painful on all of these levels. To be able to complete an Ironman, an individual must have an extremely high threshold for pain and suffering.

I see Holly from a distance. She pedals up to the dismount line with a few other racers and slowly unclicks her shoes from her clip-in pedals. She swings her leg over her bike and dismounts. As she starts to push her bike to the transition area to get ready to change clothes for her run, she doesn't look like she's in a good state of mind. Her usually tan face looks very pale and her eyes look glassy.

"Holly, you're doing really well! Keep it up! You are going to have a strong run," I yell, trying to encourage and lift her spirits.

She makes eye contact with me, but does not respond. This is unusual for her, and it troubles me. She's looking at me, but it almost seems as if she is looking straight through me.

I try again. "Holly, I love you. You look great. Keep it up."

I'm lying. She doesn't look great at this point. Holly is a beautiful woman, but she looks terrible right now. She's ghostly white, and her eyes look dilated, like they are bugging out of her head.

"Make sure to hydrate and eat a bunch," I tell her as she walks off with her bike to the changing area to get ready for the marathon she has to start running in a few minutes.

She finally speaks as she heads off to get changed, "I'm fine. I'll be alright."

It breaks my heart to see the person I love most in this world suffer like this. I think about trying to talk her into quitting for a minute, but there is no sense in this. I know how much this means to her. She's not about to quit. If she doesn't finish this race, she would have to be dragged off before she would quit.

Her four previous Ironman races were successes. She finished them all. However, I have serious doubts about her finishing this race. I've never seen her in this type of condition. She is going to have a tough time running the last 26.2 miles.

About a dozen or so minutes later, she comes out, ready to run. I'm standing on the other side of the fence, walking by her side as she makes her way to the chute to run. I motion for her to come closer. When she gets within reach, I give her a kiss on her salty forehead.

Usually when I try to coach her, she gets mad. It's kind of funny. I perform mindfulness coaching with big-time professional athletes and collegiate All-Americans, but my wife doesn't like when I try to coach her. I guess she's too tired to fight it at this point. I lean next to her ear and say, "Remember your mantra."

As she takes off into the night to start the marathon, she holds a hand over her head with five spread out fingers. FIVE is her mantra. It stands for five successfully completed Ironman triathlons. Finishing the race tonight will give her that number. This is an impressive number even to seasoned Ironmen, an astonishing feat. It means a lot to her.

As she heads off down the dark streets towards downtown Louisville, I feel much better about her chances of completing the race. It's nothing she said. It's not that she looked any better. It's the simple fact that she flashed me the five sign with her fingers. This tells me that she is locked in mentally. It also tells me that she is willing to endure the inevitable and excruciating suffering to attain her goal.

Holly does not get paid to do this. She has a good job. A loving family. Dogs. A nice, comfortable life. So the obvious question for many people is: "Why in the world would she want to endure this type of self-inflicted suffering?" I have often wondered this myself.

I have spent a good amount of time working with endurance athletes like Holly. Some are Ironmen, others are ultra marathoners, running 50- and 100-mile foot races over difficult terrain. A few have climbed Mount Kilimanjaro. Whenever I ask them what drives them to attempt these seemingly crazy adventures, most respond with, "Because I can." Sometimes I also get, "I do it because it makes me feel alive."

Holly's response to this question a few years ago after completing her third Ironman race was, "I feel that it's good to take on a task that is bigger than myself. Knowing I can get through an Ironman and succeed tells me that I can accomplish anything when I set my mind to it."

You don't have to be an Ironman or an extreme endurance athlete to understand the nature of suffering. We suffer because of our tendencies to attach (cling) to things, people, or ideas. The more we crave something, we more we suffer.

Michael Singer, the spiritual teacher and author of *The Surrender Experiment*, has a unique approach to life. He implores us to surrender to what unfolds to us in our lives. He is not suggesting that we become masochistic in our mindset and sadistically welcome suffering. Instead, he suggests that we surrender to the inevitable and let it work through us, because it is futile to senselessly resist what is transpiring in any given moment. Holly's approach to the less than desirable conditions in her race can serve as an example of the power of surrender.

Look at Holly's response when I engaged her in conversation in the bike transition pit. She said, "I'm fine. I'll be alright." She knew that fixating on the terrible conditions would not help her in her goal to finish the race. Furthermore, she knew that she had no control over these variables. She can't control the weather. She can't control that the roads on the bike course were wet and slick. So she surrendered to the moment.

Hearing her say, "I'm fine. I'll be alright," told me that Holly accepted the conditions of the present moment and that she could deal with them. I would have been more concerned with her state of mind and her ability to finish the race if she would have replied with, "This sucks. The rain and wind are killing me. The roads are slick. People wiped out all over the bike course." Even though these statements are true, it does no good to dwell on them. We are better off surrendering to what we can't control and doing the best we can in any situation.

As I have heard Michael Singer say in his presentations, "Laugh at the rain. What's the sense in getting upset with the weather? You aren't going to be able to change it." Singer is wise. Use inclement weather and other "inconveniences" as opportunities for growth on your mindfulness journey.

One mantra I've used with athletes over the years is ETS: "Embrace the Struggle." I have used this with athletes in several sports, but have found it especially helpful with golfers. I turned this phrase into a mantra after watching Tiger Woods play. I am not a golfer or really even much of a golf fan, but I always enjoyed seeing him play. Part of the reason I liked Tiger was because his mother introduced him to mindfulness and meditation at a young age. It showed in his game.

Many golfers would seem visibly upset after hitting a bad shot. Tiger was different. There were times when he would hit a terrible shot you could notice a grimace – almost a smile – on his face. This half smile on his face was saying he was not happy about shanking a shot, but he was going to make the best of it and enjoy digging out of this bad situation. That is what ETS is all about: embracing the struggle.

Resisting the struggle will only make you dig yourself a deeper hole. ETS will help you see the situation for what it is and get out of it quicker, whether it is a golf match, an Ironman triathlon, a situation at work, or a personal matter.

Obviously there are different forms of suffering and different degrees of suffering. It could be argued that the type of suffering endured by Holly in the Ironman race is a form of self-inflicted suffering, while someone fighting against a terminal disease is suffering through something they did not bring onto themselves.

While it may be difficult to feel sympathy for Tiger Woods' suffering from hitting a bad shot into a sand trap in comparison to a child suffering from inoperable brain cancer, his suffering is no less real.

We have all heard the wise old adage: "Life is not what happens to us. It is how we respond to what happens to us." The same can be said for the ways in which we respond to suffering.

Viktor Frankl, the late Austrian neurologist and psychiatrist who wrote the seminal book, *Man's Search for Meaning*, suffered unimaginable pain as much of his family was killed by the Nazis in concentration camps. Frankl was able to survive various concentration camps during the Holocaust, much in part due to his philosophy on life and his approach to suffering.

This horrific tragedy became the cornerstone for his life's work, and it helped him define his theory of Logotherapy, which was founded on the notion that we are all looking for a life purpose. Through discovering our life purposes, we can find out what life means to us.

The three principles of Logotherapy are:

1. Life has meaning under all circumstances. We can learn even from the most miserable ones.

2. Our main motivation for living is our will to find meaning in our lives.

3. We have freedom to find meaning in what we do, and what we experience, even in our suffering.

Frankl's teachings implore us that there is much to learn from our sufferings. While it is foolish and mean to intentionally cause suffering to ourselves or others, we can use unavoidable suffering as a worthwhile teacher on our journey.

True to form, Holly ended up finishing her fifth Ironman race successfully. I do believe that her ability to suffer through the tough conditions on race day and complete the race was due in large part to her ability to accept the circumstances and find meaning in her suffering.

For her next adventure, she is planning to race a 100-mile mountain bike trek up the mountains of Leadville, Colorado. Maybe she will let me coach her. I doubt it!

Chapter 10
Hold on Loosely

"Hold everything in your hands lightly, otherwise it hurts when God pries your fingers open." — *Corrie ten Boom*

In the previous chapter, we examined Holly's Ironman race as a metaphor for suffering. It should be noted that there is a big difference between "pain" and "suffering." In the Buddhist tradition, it is widely accepted that pain is an inevitable part of the human condition, but suffering does not have to be.

In other words, we can always count on having pain, but with mindfulness we can control how much suffering we endure. As Shinzen Young says, "Suffering = Pain x Resistance." This means that when we fight something we have no control over, we bring about needless suffering to ourselves.

Using Holly and her Ironman race as an example again, let's dive into this a bit. During her race, Holly's mindfulness training and background in meditation gave her skills that enabled her to have some control over the degree of her suffering. Her mantra —"FIVE" – made some of her unavoidable suffering meaningful and worthwhile. As we saw from Frankl's

Logotherapy in the last chapter, finding meaning in our suffering helps us get through it.

Holly had much pain in her Ironman race, which is understandable. Covering that kind of distance is going to beat you up. While she did suffer some, she kept much of her suffering to a minimum by acknowledging a lot of her pain instead of resisting it. For instance, when her feet and legs were very sore during the marathon at the end of the race, she acknowledged it to herself instead of resisting it. If she would have outright resisted it, it would have become worse in her mind and turned into outright suffering. By acknowledging it, she was able to not cling to it in an obsessive way. In doing so, she could work with it. Getting mad at her legs for being sore could have led to disastrous results.

As we discovered in the last chapter, the wind was brutal on the bike portion of Holly's race. It caused her much pain. She made the conscious decision to not let that pain turn into suffering by accepting the terrible condition of the wind. She leaned into this mentally instead of putting up futile mental resistance to it.

It is important to note that while Holly used her mantra of "FIVE" to give this experience meaning, she did not obsess or cling to only thinking about the finish line of the race. Mentally clinging to the finish line would have taken her out of each present moment, which would have caused needless suffering.

Instead, she used "FIVE" almost as a reminder to herself why she was doing this race. Once she reminded herself each time, she would mentally go back to the present moment, i.e., the mile she was currently on. This kind of method helps us balance meaningfulness with mindfulness. If Holly would have kept her mind just on the finish line the whole time, she would have suffered, because suffering is often rooted in being in one place physically but in a different one mentally.

There is a saying I use with my athletes: "The best way to eat an elephant is one bite at a time." If Holly were to only focus on the finish line, she would be embarking on the impossible task of swallowing the entire elephant in one bite. By reminding herself occasionally why she wanted to eat the elephant and then returning to the task of chewing up the elephant slowly, she was more successful. Clinging too hard to the thought of just the finish line would have made each mile of the race a miserable experience for her.

One way to minimize our suffering is to be more conscious of our mental clinging. This helps us to stop doing it. Think about how much you cling to things mentally over which you have no control. We all do it.

Most of us start clinging at a young age. I remember looking forward to Christmas weeks before the holiday every year. I would start my countdown two weeks in advance. While I always loved the holiday, it never lived up to the unrealistic expectations my clinging conjured up in my mind. Now that I look back in retrospect, I think about all of the weeks of my life I wasted waiting for that day to come over the years.

We do the same with vacations as adults. When we have some time off and a great trip planned, we cling to it and obsess over it for months in advance. Not only does it seldom live up to the hype in our heads, but we also cling during the actual vacation. On day four of a seven day trip, you catch yourself worrying, "I only have three more days left of this vacation." You do this every day of the vacation. It diminishes your ability to fully enjoy this experience.

I had a girlfriend in college I was crazy about. Because our class schedules did not jibe and she had a part-time job after school, we were only able to spend an hour or so together on most days. I spent most of my time back then worrying about not getting to see her. She would call me every night on the dorm payphone about 9 p.m. This was before the time of mobile phones! I would crack open my room door about 8:30 and start waiting for the phone to ring. When I look back now, I cringe! I wasted so much time and effort clinging to this situation. Instead, I should have just been enjoying her company when we were together.

Sometimes the sagest advice comes to us from the most bizarre sources. I heard a song on the radio the other day that made me think of this. It comes from a Southern rock band called *.38 Special*. Their song *Hold On Loosely* was a big hit in the 80's. I think that the key for us to avoid suffering from clinging is to hold on to what is important to us *loosely*. If we squeeze too tightly, we will obsess about the future or ruminate in the past. This will take us out of the present moment and make us miserable. By all means, hang on to what you value, but give it some wiggle room. Don't pass up the precious present moments of life by clinging to what may or may not happen.

What situations, experiences, ideas, emotions, or people are you clinging too much to? Are you clinging too tightly to your desire for a promotion at work? Are you clinging too much to your child's academic success or prowess on the athletic fields? Maybe you are clinging so much to making as much money as possible you are missing out on enjoying your job. Perhaps you are replaying a past incident or experience too much in your mind. Woulda. Shoulda. Coulda.

Whenever I do laundry, I try to remember to use a dryer sheet to remove the static cling. See mindfulness as your dryer sheet to get rid of the clinging. Insert it into everything you do. By all means, set your goals and intentions. Go after them, but hold on loosely, because having too tight a mental grip on everything we do and experience will cause us to suffer.

Chapter 11
One

"So then, the relationship of self to other is the complete realization that loving yourself is impossible without loving everything defined as other than yourself." — Alan Watts

I love flying into a city at night. As I look out of the airplane window below, it is dark. I am mesmerized by the lights. Gazing down on a city at night makes things seem peaceful. The cars, with their lights shining, look like tiny little ants marching. It looks like they are all in a row, lined up, carrying out a common cause. From this distance, there seems to be a harmony to the movement. It is almost as if you can feel the vibrant energy. Distances between cars, homes, and buildings from my vantage point up here seem nonexistent. In some ways it seems like a living, breathing organism with different parts working together in unison, all interconnected. The gentle buzzing noise from the plane sets a nice soundtrack to the picture, almost as if the little cars below have a rhythm of their own, keeping them in sync.

A peaceful easy feeling comes over me as I look out, and then I remember a passage from a book that reminds me of this. When I taught high school English years ago, one of my favorite passages was from John Steinbeck's novella, *The Pearl*. The first sentence in Chapter 3 this classic piece of literature starts off: *"A town is a thing like a colonial animal. A town has a nervous system and a head and shoulders and feet."*

In a much grander sense, astronauts have described this same sense of our interconnectedness when viewing the Earth from orbit. From space (similar to my airplane view), boundaries are broken down. Some believe what the astronauts experience in these instances is a cognitive shift in awareness. Since the boundaries are broken down, conflicts dividing people seem less significant from outer space. In fact, some astronauts claim they have been profoundly changed by this experience. It has made many of them realize that there is no true separation between us all. Astronaut Chris Hadfield summed it up by saying: "If anything, because our whole planet was just outside the window, I felt even more aware of and connected to the seven billion other people who call it home."

When working with teams, I have often told coaches that a team is like an organism. The coach is the brain. The assistant coaches and staff are the nervous system. The players are the various body parts. This organism must have all body parts working together in order to "be healthy" – to reach maximum potential. The parts of the body (players) are very symbiotic. In other words, they feed off the actions, language, emotions, and motion of the brain (coach) and nervous system (assistant coaches). If one part of the body is acting up or "sick," especially the brain or nervous system, the rest of the body suffers. In essence, when this happens, no one wins.

A few weeks ago, I was at a college basketball team's practice. Before practice started, I led the team through a meditation.

As practice begins, any chance of them hanging on to any chill vibes from the session are erased in about thirty seconds. As soon as they hit the gym floor, their coaches and staff members are barking at them. The head coach, a good friend of mine, had given me a warning in advance. "We aren't going to be too mindful today," he'd chuckled as he walked out and blew his whistle. He was pissed off because they dropped a game two days ago to a team they should have beaten.

The assistant coaches, sensing he was pissed, are pacing the sidelines, yelling at the players at the top of their lungs. Whistles are being blown like crazy to a deafening tone. The scene is thick in the gym. The nervous energy is palpable, testosterone in overdrive!

Players are shown no mercy. After any little mistake, they are yelled at and immediately ordered to either run full-speed sprints, hop on a stationary bike and peddle like crazy, or go like a madman on the VersaClimber for a little extra, intense cardio as a consequence.

I understand what the coach is doing. The team played poorly in their defeat. You could even say they played rather complacently and sloppily. The coach is teaching them a lesson on how not to overlook opponents. I get where he is coming from. However, the scene is still a bit nerve-racking to me, a guy who doesn't spend every afternoon in a gym!

This is a big-time program. So when a team gets upset in a game like this, they get hammered by fans and the media. In essence, losing a game to a team you are supposed to easily beat is hard on the entire "organism." The players have looks on their faces ranging from disgust and apathy to simple sadness. Their body language is sad as well, with most of their shoulders slumped, and their movements suggesting dejection. The coach looks angry and agitated. The assistant coaches seem nervous. Just being around this vibe is stressful to me!

The young man who missed the shot that would have won the game looks especially tense, which is understandable. I feel for him. He is an outstanding young man.

As practice draws to its conclusion, the coach gets them in a huddle and gives them some words of encouragement. They put their hands together and chant "ONE" before breaking the huddle. "ONE" is one of the mantras we use. It stands for one team, one breath at a time, one shot at a time, and the overall power of one. We made a conscious effort to play as one functioning unit, the "organism."

As the players scatter from the gym to the locker room, a half-dozen or so, including the player who missed the shot, come up to me and ask if I would lead them in a meditation. "Will you breathe with us, Coach?" one of them asks.

These young men range in age from 18-23, but to me, they are young boys. Fans see them as machines or invincible athletes, but to a guy my age, they are babies. They are still developing in all phases of maturation. They have a tremendous amount of responsibility and stress on them. I cannot imagine dealing with all that they do at their age.

We get to the film room, and I shut the door and turn off the overhead light. There is a small lamp on in the corner. They close their eyes and sit up straight. My eyes are open as I began to lead them through the breathing exercise.

As they begin to focus on their breath, they seem to loosen up. We dive in and find a brief respite from the chaos and madness. After a few minutes, their breathing seems to collectively find the same rhythm. It is as if they are breathing as "one."

A calm expression finds each face, one by one. A lone tear rolls slowly down the cheek of the young man who missed the shot. It is heartbreaking and peaceful at the same time.

While I am sitting there, I realize that ONE is much more than just a mantra. We are all ONE. We are all more connected than we realize. We all have more similarities than differences.

It is not only people who are connected as one. Everything in the universe is connected. Thich Nhat Hanh describes our connectedness beautifully with his concept of Interbeing. *He basically says that each and every object and/or phenomenon in the universe is dependent on all others for survival.*

When we are aware that everyone and everything in our universe is connected, we are in a better frame of mind to receive the world as it truly is, and to be mindful. There is no victory without defeat. There is no joy without pain. There is no life without death. It is all connected.

The late Richard Feynman, who was a well-respected theoretical physicist, brilliantly articulated our interconnectedness by saying, "I, a universe of atoms, an atom in the universe."

We cling too much to our sense of self. The ego drives us to continue clinging to "I" and "Me." This makes an illusion of separateness between us and all other being and things. Conscious breathing and meditation give us a break from this madness. It lets us see how our minds play crazy tricks on us. We discover that we don't need to cling to anything not genuine to our being. Doing so only puts up more separation from others. This causes pain.

Few things worthwhile have ever been accomplished solo, without the support of others. While most of us are probably aware of this, we often, for unknown reasons, continue to swim upstream by trying to take on the world individually. There is strength when we realize that we are all connected more than we are separated.

As my mind comes back to the meditation with the players, I look at their peaceful faces and decide that they will all be fine. A few of them may end up playing in the NBA. The vast majority will not. At this moment, as their breathing is in sync, they will all be fine.

The timer on my phone rings, and they all open their eyes and stand up slowly. On the way out the door, the short point guard gives the tall center who missed the shot a big hug. They may have lost on the scoreboard, but they all won today. They are ONE. It's a beautiful thing.

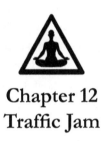

Chapter 12
Traffic Jam

*"You are not stuck in traffic.
You ARE traffic." —Anonymous*

Is there anything worse than being stuck in a traffic jam? Few things in life are more stressful. Heavy traffic can often bring out the worst in us. Do you ever notice how one minute you can be in your car happily singing to the radio and the next moment you are enraged at the driver who is driving too slowly in front of you or furious at the person who almost ran you off the road with his reckless NASCAR wanna-be driving style? In a matter of seconds, you go from being happy to turning into the Incredible Hulk.

How about when you are running late on your morning commute and you get stuck behind a very slow moving log truck or school bus? How do you feel? Do you ever realize that the little voice in your head – that's your ego – automatically labels almost anyone driving slower than you an "idiot" and anyone driving way too fast for your tastes a "jerk" (or worse)?

Do you ever notice the emotions and physical sensations that may arise from driving in a traffic jam or in a heavy traffic morning commute? Perhaps you get caught by a stop light. In any other circumstance, you're a mild-mannered, friendly individual, but this particular traffic light turning red at this particular moment is going to make you late to an important meeting with your boss. You stomp on the gas to pass the light, but then you hesitate as it turns yellow, realizing you aren't going to make it. You freeze for a second, then you slam on the brake and your overpriced cup of coffee spills all over your brand new outfit. Forgetting your kids are in the back seat, you unleash a stream of profanities. You can feel your heart beating out of your chest. Your palms are sweaty. Your kids, who are frightened, are now crying. How does this happen? One minute you are singing along with Maroon 5 on the radio at the top of your lungs without a care in the world, and everything is hunky dory. The next minute you are slamming on the break, dropping F-bombs in front of the kids and hating life in general!

Your blood pressure is rising and your heart rate is through the roof. What are you going to do? You need to drop your kids off to school and rush into work to make the meeting on time, but then this light has the audacity to turn red! What's going on here? If this is how the first hour of your day starts off, can you imagine how the rest of your day is going to be?

Even if you live in an urban environment where you take the subway and don't have a morning drive to work, you get the picture. You know what I'm talking about. This is how many of us live, subservient to our thoughts and emotions.

There is a better way to live.

The truth is that our minds are wonderful devices for assisting with our survival, but they are terrible at making us happy. We have these things that occupy the streets of our minds called thoughts, and just like cars and other vehicles traveling like mad on morning commutes on superhighways, our thoughts dash in and out and often congest the roads of our minds. Outside in the real word there is always some kind of commotion coming from traffic. Our inner-traffic is no different – so much confusion and noise, always speeding through our minds.

Guess what? You are never going to stop the traffic on the highway. The same holds true for the traffic in your head. You are never going to stop it, but you can learn to deal with it.

Jon-Kabat Zinn, the godfather of Western mindfulness, has a wonderful quote about thoughts: "You can't stop the waves, but you can learn to surf." Let's take a look at our minds, the way our thoughts work, and how to deal with the waves and the traffic.

Scientists have long debated and disagreed over how many thoughts we have during a 24-hour period, but estimates usually range from 50,000 to 70,000 thoughts per day. Using the higher figure, that averages to about 49 thoughts per minute. I don't believe there is any way to know that exact number, but for argument's sake, there is a ton of traffic circulating around your mind and honking for your attention at any given time.

Do you ever notice that the vast majority of your 49 thoughts per minute are either ruminating in the past or worrying about the future? Typically, we are fixated quite a bit with what we perceive is just around the corner. Most of the time, we worry about things that never happen. This is because our minds are wired to protect us from these perceived threats. We were created (or programmed) with a fight, flight, or freeze survival instinct. This response system was helpful when we lived in prehistoric hunter and gather communities, but is less vital, in terms of practical survival, in today's sedentary digital age. We have a physical response (rapid heartbeat, sweaty palms) and mental response (racing thoughts) to any perceived threat. This was helpful in prehistoric days when a violent tribe was attacking our huts. It's not so helpful when we are on our morning drive to work in our Prius.

Instead of dwelling in the past or obsessing about the future, our true happiness lies in our ability to be fully engaged in the present moment. The past is dead, and it's not coming back. Dwelling in the past is like chaining a dead animal to your foot and dragging it around. Why on earth would you do this? Furthermore, the future is usually just a fantasy. Why would you want to hang out there? As we learned from Marty McFly in *Back to the Future*, nothing good happens there.

The present moment is the only reality you have. The whole essence of mindfulness is about getting stuck in the present moment. Mindfulness is about living in the present moment without judgement (or as little judgement as you can have). Living in the present moment does not mean you ignore the past and the future. By all means, you learn from the past, and you plan for the future. However, you do not need to be a slave to either the past or the future in the highways of your mind.

What really helps is to start thinking about your thinking. This begins with the way in which we see our thoughts. Descartes uttered the famous lines, "I think, therefore I am." From a mindfulness perspective, I don't like this quote. Anyone can and does think. The key is knowing when not to think and to not be bossed around by the constant traffic in your mind.

Contrary to Descartes' emphasis on the thinking mind, author Simon Boylan has a profound quote which implores us to pay less attention to those 49 thoughts every minute and instead focus on what happens between one thought and the next: "Everything you ever needed to know is waiting in the space between your thoughts."

The first step in learning to slow down the traffic in your mind is to start seeing your thoughts as mental activity, not absolute truths. Say it over and over in your head: "Thoughts are mental activity, not absolute truths."

Just like running and jumping are physical activities, thoughts are mental activity. It is important to realize that you are not your thoughts. Start seeing yourself as the observer of your thoughts. Getting in the habit of doing this will enable you to ease much of the suffering from your anxious and self-doubting thoughts.

It is important to note that you will always have anxious and self-doubting thoughts to some extent. It is the ego's job to do this. Remember, the mind is good at protecting us from perceived threats, but not so good at making us happy. Don't hate the ego; just bring awareness to what it is saying. By "calling it out," it dissipates, and the voice will eventually stop. By being able to stop it after a while, we don't ruminate in it and become enslaved by our negative thoughts. This enables us to make more mindful, rational decisions.

There is a difference between simply acknowledging what our ego is saying at any given time and trying to mentally resist what the ego is saying. Have you ever tried not to think about something? What happens? It makes you think about it more! Mental resistance will only make negative thoughts stronger. Instead of trying to fight what is going on in your mind, bring gentle awareness to it and acknowledge what it is saying.

Bringing awareness to what is going on in your mind also brings you back to the present moment. Instead of getting stuck in your thoughts and going down the deep, dark rabbit holes of the past and the future, you are alert and thriving in the present moment. You can actually function in the present moment, unlike the past or the future.

Don't stop with just bringing awareness to your thoughts. Also do it with your feelings and emotions as well. In this regard, mindfulness will help you develop better emotional intelligence. When you get angry, acknowledge it. Say to yourself, "I'm mad," and deal with it, instead of blowing up at something or someone. It's better to acknowledge a feeling or emotion instead of blowing up or overreacting and regretting your actions later. Do it when you are sad, mad, scared, or jealous. Make it a habit. You will be able to unclog much of the traffic in your mind this way, and it will get you back into your destination: the present moment.

The next time you are running late and get caught by a traffic light (either real or imagined), take a moment to get centered and back to the present moment by trying the S.T.O.P. practice:

S: Stop what you are doing

T: Take a breath (or several)

O: Observe what is going on (inside and out)

P: Proceed

If you like the S.T.O.P. practice and find it helpful, consider integrating it into your driving routine. It can be your traffic meditation every time you come to a red light or stop sign.

I worked with a coach who was always running from task to task. As you can imagine, he was under a microscope, as he was a high-profile figure, and his enormous fan base and media had high expectations. We worked together to develop a plan for him to incorporate "pockets of stillness" into his work day. His plan entailed him turning off his lights and shutting his office door several times per day and simply sitting still and focusing on how his breath rising and falling. He viewed these mini, brief one- to three-minute sessions as opportunities to get his ruminating mind still, where he could streamline his thoughts and get focused. Focusing on his breath rising and falling took his attention off the constant swirling mental clutter in is head. He attributes much of his success to these sessions.

Even if you don't have a fancy office or a private place to curb your mental traffic, you can still utilize this method to work in some "mini-meditations" or "mindful moments." The beauty of mindfulness is that it is portable. You don't even need to tether yourself to a smartphone charger or plug-in.

I try to use traffic jams, red lights, and other similar daily occurrences as opportunities to return to the present moment. Instead of looking at them as obstacles, aggravations, or hindrances, why don't you try a mindset shift, and instead see them as a chance to get centered and grounded? View these this way, and there will be a paradigm shift in the way you think and feel. You will be amazed at how liberating it can be. Places like the grocery store, the dry cleaner, your place of work, and the drive-through line can be places to practice cultivating your inner-peace. You spend more time in these places than anywhere else, so why not chose to turn a potentially frustrating encounter or experience into something uplifting? Use them to your advantage.

When the clerk at the grocery store checkout isn't fast enough and it seems to be taking forever to get checked out, take a deep breath or two (in and out of your nose) and realize that there are worse things in life that a slow checkout line. Make eye contact with the clerk. Ask her how she is doing. The present moment affords us many opportunities like this to connect and engage with others. In doing so, not only do we feel better, we spark that same feeling in those with whom we interact.

Next time the guy at the dry cleaner counter can't find your ticket, practice keeping your cool. See your time at the counter while he is looking for your ticket as a moment during which you can slow down your inner-traffic. Collect your thoughts. Check in with your breathing. Your breath is a barometer for your emotional state; it tells you a lot about your stress level. Is it tight and restricted, or is it easy flowing and loose? Observe your breath while the clerk is looking for your ticket. If you need to, take a few deep breaths to get some oxygen to your brain, and get your breathing into a slow, steady cadence.

We often create traffic jams in our minds by believing we are good at multitasking. This is a myth. As a species, we are terrible at multitasking. Instead of doing a good job on a task, we often spread ourselves too thin by trying to focus on too many things at once. By doing so, we do a mediocre job on several fronts instead of doing an excellent job on one thing at a time. Practice being mindful at work by bringing your full attention to the task at hand. Enjoy the moment fully when you cross things off of your to-do list one item at a time.

Make a conscious effort not to be in a hurry all of the time. Like John Lennon sang: "Life is what happens when we are busy making plans."

We spend so much of our lives rushing around and fixating on what's next. Make the most of the time you have by enjoying every moment to the fullest.

Chapter 13
Dodgeball

"Between stimulus and response there is a space. In that space is our power to choose our response. In our response lies our growth and our freedom." — Viktor Frankl

It is kind of ironic that I spend my daytime hours as a middle school principal, because as a kid I did not like much about middle school. In fact, there were only two things I liked about it: lunch and gym class. The best thing about lunch was square pizza day, and the best thing about gym class were the days when we were allowed to play dodgeball.

Do you remember playing dodgeball as a kid in gym class? If not, I truly feel sorry for you. Dodgeball is the game where two teams are positioned on separate ends of the gym, and they try to hit each other with rubber balls. When a person is hit, he or she is out. Players can also get someone out by catching the ball that was thrown at them. Being agile and having the ability to dodge and catch the fast moving balls is a real advantage – hence the term "dodgeball."

It was often brutal, but it was so much fun. I must admit, I loved it. There were always the big, athletic kids in the class who could throw the ball really hard. These guys were punishers, as their strong throws would often inflict pain and embarrassment. There were also quick-thinking kids who would focus successfully on the throws and dodge the speeding balls with extreme dexterity and grace.

There was a real thrill for most of us playing this game, a feeling somewhere between excitement and fear. At any given moment in a dodgeball match you could end up being a hero or a buffoon, depending on whether you smacked someone in the head with a ball or you were the one who got smacked.

I have never done any significant research on the matter, but I am firmly convinced that the smack talking which runs so prevalent in sports today could be traced back to middle school gym class dodgeball matches of the 1970s. We would razz each other for weeks about getting creamed with the ball in the face and chant for our classmates to "kill" each other. Nothing elicited more laughter that some dude's glasses flying through the air from the smack of a rubber ball on the noggin. It was like *Lord of the Flies* in Chuck Taylor canvas sneakers and ill-fitting P.E. uniform shorts!

In retrospect, I think the P.E. teachers let us play dodgeball for their own personal entertainment. They would sit around and watch us, giggling, heckling us, and cheering us on. Coach Sheib, the boys' coach who looked like one of the Mario Brothers with a limp, would sometimes join in on the action and toss a ball or two at us from time to time. The girls' coach, Coach Goodwin, was a dead ringer for the mean-spirited P.E. teacher from the now defunct TV show Glee, Sue Sylvester. As if the perils of adolescence and puberty for middle school boys weren't bad enough on their own merits, Coach Goodwin would hurl the nastiest insults at us while we tried to pulverize each other!

The game has come under much scrutiny in recent years. Many school districts have banned the game from their physical education class curriculum, citing the violent and uncivil nature of the game. In fact, as a school principal I made the tough decision to ban it at our school, despite my nostalgic fondness for it. The game seems to be dying a slow death, despite a brief resurgence in its popularity several years back with Ben Stiller's hilarious *Dodgeball* movie.

I use dodgeball as a metaphor to explain the concept of mindfulness to people I work with sometimes. Not to sound Forrest Gump-ish, but life really is like dodgeball. Like rubber balls whizzing by our heads at a feverish pace in a dodgeball game, life often throws stuff at us. We always seem to have difficult thoughts, emotions, situations, and experiences hurling at us from all directions.

The best dodgers in dodgeball were not the guys who hunkered down in the corner of the gym with their hands over their heads in the fetal position in an attempt to avoid getting hit. These guys always got smacked worse, as they were sitting ducks. The guys who were able to focus on the balls really well usually ended up winning the game. They usually weren't the most athletic guys, and they knew this. They were the guys who paid attention and kept their minds on the balls. By doing this, they overcome lack of athleticism with concentration. They were able to stay in the present moment and do the best with what they had to work with. This is the essence of mindfulness.

Life often comes at us fast and furious. Sometimes we are the ones throwing the balls. Sometimes we are the ones having balls thrown at us. We cannot control what balls are being heaved at us. However, we can learn over time how to keep our eyes on the ball and how to respond. I go back to that overused cliché: "Life isn't what happens to us. It's how we respond." It sounds trite, but it's true.

Notice I used the word "respond," not "react." There is an important distinction here. When we react, we are simply trying to avoid getting hit out of fear, almost on reflex. When we respond, we are moving in a proactive way to either avoid getting hit, or we are moving to catch the ball.

We are never going to be able to stop difficult or unpleasant experiences or situations from being thrown at us in life. So we must cultivate self-awareness. Being self-aware gives us a superpower. By being self-aware, we learn what is going on inside of us both mentally and emotionally. Self-awareness is arguably the most important by-product we develop through a mindfulness practice.

From a dodgeball perspective, when we are self-aware, we are alert and know where we are in relation to the balls being thrown at us. When we are not self-aware, we are not operating from a mindful mindset. It's just the opposite. Instead, we are operating from a mindless mindset. When we are mindless, we are so afraid of getting hit by the ball that we lose our wits and end up acting out of nervous energy or fear-based angst. In doing so, we are more likely to spazz out and get pounded in the head by the ball.

I am not suggesting that you try to dodge every difficult thought, emotion, situation, or experience that is thrown your way. Just the opposite. I am urging you to be aware of what is coming your way. Keep your eyes on the ball, so to speak. Stay alert and focused. Try and notice what is going on both inside and outside of yourself. Bringing awareness to what is going on in our minds is much different than obsessing over it.

My approach is threefold: 1. Try to bring awareness to what is bothering you. 2. If you can make it better, deal with it. 3. If not, let it go.

One of the best ways to cultivate self-awareness is to get into the habit of recognizing your triggers. What or who sets you off or makes you worry? If you are self-aware enough to realize this, you won't let it bother you as much. By doing this, you are keeping your eye on the ball instead of being smacked by it.

If someone or something triggers you, learn to be proactive about it. Learn how to deal with him, her, or it. Don't cower down in the corner of the gym and get smacked by that dodgeball. Be ready for it before it comes your way. Deal with it. Dodge it or catch it.

There are times when we all get smacked by the dodgeball. We all have blind spots. A blind spot is a habit or a way of behaving that everyone knows about you, except you. Start getting into the practice of trying to recognize and embrace these blind spots.

If you have no idea what your blind spots are, ask those who are close to you. It may be difficult to hear at first, but it will be very helpful to find out what they are, so you can work on filling them in. Before too long with work, self-awareness will prevail and your blind spots will be less prevalent. The more aware you are of your surroundings and yourself, the less often you will have to deal with getting smacked in the head.

If the dodgeball metaphor doesn't work for you, be thankful I didn't use my other one about climbing the rope in gym class!

Chapter 14
The Zombie Apocalypse

"It has become appallingly obvious that our technology has exceeded our humanity." — Albert Einstein

I must confess, I look at my smartphone too much. Even though my lectures on mindful living usually touch on the downside of the over-reliance on technology, I still struggle with this from time to time. I am, however, making a conscious effort to not look at my phone as much.

It's kind of funny if you think about it. Technology is something we created to make our lives easier. It's supposed to save us time and effort. However, quite often, tech enslaves us and becomes a colossal time suck. All of the research I uncover on this subject tells me that we should all try to refrain from using tech more than we need to.

A recent study by Microsoft revealed that the average goldfish has an attention span of nine seconds. No big deal, right? It is no big deal...unless you consider that that average person has an eight second attention span! This is unacceptable. No offense to goldfish, but you don't want to be one of them.

There is great irony in a tech company like Microsoft sponsoring this type of study. This study revealed that the average attention span was fifteen seconds in the year 2000. It dropped to eight seconds in 2015. It is a safe assumption to make that our dependence on tech has played a major role in our ever-decreasing attention span and our struggle to successfully sustain focus. As writer and artist Debby Millman so profoundly states, we live in a "140 character culture." In other words, we want everything fast and expressed in 140 characters or less.

I did some research a few years ago on the state of our decreasing attention spans and discovered that a radio station in Calgary was only playing half of each song. That's right! Amp Radio was the first to go to this "Quickhitz" format, cutting top 40 songs in half in an attempt not to "bore its listeners." So much for FM long-form standards like "Freebird" and "Aqualung!"

As a society, we spend too much time living in the cyber world of artificial intelligence. We aren't comfortable just *being*. Instead of just being alone with our thoughts and emotions, our first instinct is to pull out our phones and entertain or distract ourselves.

Constantly checking a smartphone becomes an addiction, because doing so can actually increase the level of dopamine in your brain. With this in mind, the Chinese media has coined a term for our addiction to all things tech – "digital heroin." It's scary.

Go to any restaurant, coffee shop, or doctor's office and observe this phenomenon. People don't even read magazines in waiting rooms anymore. If you would have told someone in 1955 that we carry around small pocket computers in our pockets or purses with all of the information in the history of humankind at the touch of a button, they would be astonished. It's too bad we often use them for jackassery. Instead of reading a book and using our brains or just sitting with ourselves in the present moment, we watch monkey videos and check our social media accounts to see how many "likes" we have accrued.

Even when we are in the company of loved ones or friends, we display this same type of behavior. The fatal attraction to our devices I'm describing here is nothing new. This excerpt comes from an article I wrote on March 22, 2007, for the *Memphis Flyer* weekly newspaper:

> For instance, sitting in Huey's Midtown, I saw the strangest thing, and it left me with the impression that folks just don't talk to each other like they used to. In a booth behind us, a man was with his girlfriend. They were a nice, clean-cut, respectable-looking young couple. Initially, he was on his cellphone having a conversation while she sat there looking bored and sad and ignored. As soon as he got off his phone, she picked

hers up and started talking to someone. Now it was his turn to look sad, bored, and ignored. As soon as she ended her conversation, he picked up his phone and called someone. This went on and on and on. They took turns, volleying back and forth. I don't think they actually spoke one word to each other the entire duration of their meal. It was surreal, almost like a Fellini film. In retrospect, I think one of them should have stayed at home, and the other should have gone to the restaurant. At least that way, they would have spoken to each other.

The excerpt from the article above was written in 2007, well over a decade ago. Sadly, this phenomenon has increased exponentially. The word "phubbing" (meaning being snubbed by a smartphone) has even entered into our modern vernacular.

It seems that we are more interested in documenting our lives than actually living our lives. Go to any sporting event, art museum, or concert. What are most of the people doing? Instead of actually soaking in the experience and experiencing it with our senses, we are trying to capture it on our smartphones by snapping pictures or shooting videos. Think about this. We are experiencing it through the lens of artificial intelligence.

Don't get me wrong. There is nothing wrong with capturing some memorable moments on our phones. However, when we miss out on much of an experience because we are too busy trying to record it, then we are not being mindful. Our attention and mental output becomes fixated on getting everything captured on the phone instead of being fully in the present moment. We end up watching most of the event through the phone instead of soaking it up with our mind and senses.

While every age demographic is represented in this obsession with tech, it seems to start at an early age. Babies are given iPads instead of teddy bears or dolls to play with. It's like free babysitting. Cram a device in a kid's face, and that child is entertained for hours. Try carrying on a conversation with a young child while he or she is bathed in the glow of one of these devices. You will be severely disappointed.

As a school principal, I see the ill-effects of teens spending too much time on social media. Important socialization skills fall to the wayside as kids would rather look at Snapchat or Instagram instead of carrying on face-to-face conversations.

Over the years, I have also noticed that conflict resolution skills are seriously lacking. I attribute this to their lack of skill development in this domain, as they spend much more time interacting though devices than in person. In her book, *iGen*, Dr. Jean Twenge reveals that the average 12th grader spends an alarming six hours per day texting, on the internet, and on social media.

From a cognitive perspective, I truly believe that very few of us read with much depth or breadth these days. Unlike reading a book, reading from a device offers us all kinds of side distractions. To quote Matthew Rehrl, M.D. on the subject, "Clicking, scrolling, and swiping are the antithesis of deep thinking." I enjoy reading books on my Kindle, but I make a conscious effort to read a "real" book from time to time. Research also shows that talking notes by hand helps us remember the material better than typing it on a keyboard.

The infatuation with tech devices and social media is not limited to the young ones. Gramps and Grammy are getting into the action as well! They are all over Facebook snooping on everyone. They don't post, like, or comment on anyone's posts, but they sure know what is going on in everyone's lives! It's amazing that Grandpa went from a simple flip phone just a couple of years ago, and now he's the king of social media. And let's not even talk about crazy ole Uncle Eddie and all of his politically insensitive posts! We all have a crazy uncle.

All kidding aside, it is almost like a cheesy horror movie. We could call it the *Zombie Apocalypse*. Go anywhere and watch people in a crowd. Most are looking down at their phones, not paying attention where they are going, walking slowly – like zombies! It's almost as if the machines are eating our brains.

Dr. Nancy Colier, the author of the magnificent book, *The Power of Off: The Mindful Way to Stay Sane in a Virtual World*, offers us some staggering statistics and insights:

- The average person spends more than eight hours per day on their smartphone or laptop. This is more time than most people sleep.

- Young adults average more than 100 text messages per day.

- 46% of smartphone users say they "can't live without it."

- Most people check their smartphones at least 150 times per day.

- The smartphone is a "Trojan horse," as it sneaks work into the house.

- The average person spends 13 hours per week checking or working on email.

- 70% of children think their parents spend too much time on their devices.

- The average person spends 12 hours per day staring at a screen (computer, phone, tv, etc.).

The negatives of our collective tech addiction are not just psychological or emotionally based. There are physical consequences for being glued to our phones so much. The *New York Times* and other reputable publications have been publishing stories recently about the widespread epidemic of "Tech Neck Syndrome." This comes the constant downward craning of our necks while we are staring at our smartphones. Symptoms include: upper back or neck pain, nagging sharp pains in the neck or shoulders at the end of the day, and constant headaches.

Not only are our gadgets impacting our necks. They are hurting our love lives as well. A 2013 study of mobile consumer habits revealed that one in ten Americans use smartphones during sex! A similar study found that one-third of Americans prefer their smartphones over sex. Wow!

Technology is not going away. In fact, it has many useful benefits in our modern society. However, as with most things, a little bit goes a long way. We need to be conscious of our digital lives and make an effort to power down certain times a day. Our ancient brains have a difficult time keeping up with the rapid speed of our devices. In addition, I believe that our overreliance on technology is in part due to our inability or unwillingness to deal with our own thoughts.

What is the first thing you do when you jump into your car? I bet you turn on the radio. You probably listen to some music or even a talk radio station. Nothing is wrong with this, but do you ever give yourself time to think or sort out your own thoughts? Maybe you jump into your car every day and listen to the same political talk radio shows or maybe even sports talk jocks. Perhaps you listen to recorded books or podcasts on your commute. Again, nothing is wrong with this. However, what would happen though if instead of filling your car up immediately with noise, you take a few minutes on your drive to collect your thoughts? After a while, you will start to enjoy these moments of silence. I guarantee you that your mind will start craving these slivers of silence.

As a school principal, one of the reasons I banned the popular Fidget Spinners was because I noticed our students were using them as a distraction; a child's equivalent to the adult's smartphone. Kids pulled them out when they were bored or when they didn't want to tend to the present moment. I fear these toys are just another way for individuals to avoid dealing with their thoughts. As a society, we seem to have an aversion to simply being. We have to be doing, even if the doing is just playing with a Fidget Spinner or scrolling through social media on a cell phone. We are a society that is afraid to be bored.

Parents seem to think it is the worst thing in the world for a child to be bored. To avoid their children from being bored, parents often thrust a device in their faces. In doing this, we are robbing children from cultivating skills in which they can create, imagine, and entertain themselves. By thrusting the device in their faces, we are teaching children to fear their own company. In a recent article in *Psychology Today* entitled "Can I Let My Child Be Bored?," Dr. Colier says: "In boredom lies the possibility that we ourselves can become a worthy destination of our own attention." Simply put, let your kids be bored.

The extent to which individuals were driven not to be bored or have to deal with their own thoughts was revealed in a recent study conducted by Timothy Wilson at the University of Virginia. In his study, Wilson recruited hundreds of undergraduates and students to take part in an experiment. During the experiment, subjects were to sit alone in a room. They were given the choice to just sit there and do nothing or they could press a button to shock themselves with electricity. 67 percent of men and 25 percent of women chose to shock themselves! This illustrates our discomfort with just being alone with our thoughts. In essence, some people prefer mindlessness to mindfulness.

The good news is that there is beginning to be a bit of a backlash on the over-reliance we have on our tech devices. In February of 2018, The Center for Humane Technology announced it was releasing a widespread advertising campaign called "Truth About Tech." The objective is to educate people about how dangerous all screen time is, not just smartphones. Eighth graders who frequently use social media and smartphones are 56 percent more likely to report being unhappy, 27 percent more likely to be diagnosed as depressed, and 35 percent more likely to be at a higher risk for suicide.

One important component of maintaining a mindfulness practice is being conscious of how much time you spend on your devices. I have a few suggestions:

1.   Try not to get on your smartphone first thing in the morning. Take your time waking up. Let your mind wake up naturally without stimulation from your electronic devices.

2.   If possible, do not use your devices right before going to bed. Give yourself a tech-free hour to wind down before bed.

3.   Do not sleep next to your phone. If possible, charge it in another room while you sleep.

4.   Have certain times during the day when you power down. Make these times a habit.

5.   Have a "tech sabbatical" once a week. Some people do it for a full day (maybe a Saturday or Sunday). If a full day doesn't work for you, do it for half a day or even for just a few hours.

6.   Be conscious of the time you spend on your tech devices.

7.   Every now and then, intentionally leave your devices indoors when you go outside to have fun.

8.   Have a family agreement that tech devices will not be permitted at the table during meal times.

Chapter 15
Jumping In

"The secret of getting ahead is getting started." — Mark Twain

On several occasions I trained to run a marathon, but could not seem to make it to the starting line. I would make it through each training cycle, which would last for months, and then back out before running the race. There was always a reason I gave myself for backing out: I had not trained hard enough, or I had a minor injury, or I had a calendar conflict on race day. Deep in my heart, I knew these excuses were baseless. I was letting my mind talk me out of doing it.

From time to time, most of us suffer from "analysis paralysis." In trying to protect us, sometimes our minds go overboard and talk us out of things we want to do or need to do. I believe it is our natural instinct to instantly choose comfort over growth. If we work to realize this, we can work through it and learn to push through analysis paralysis and opt for growth. Sometimes it is as simple as just jumping in.

After completing a handful of half marathons each, Holly and I had both signed up for the San Antonio Marathon several years ago. It was going to be our first full marathon, and we were going to run it together. A couple of weeks before the race, my mind started kicking in with doubtful, self-defeating thoughts. True to form, once again, I had talked myself out of doing the marathon. Per the race rules, a runner racing the full marathon could drop back and do the half. The electronic chip timing makes this possible. I decided this is what I would do. Essentially, I would chicken out again.

I mentioned this to Holly, and she did not say much. I could tell she was not pleased with this, but she kept it to herself.

On race day, as we were walking up to the starting corral, I told Holly that I would meet her at the hotel after the race, since I would be done a few hours before her, since she was doing the 26.2 mile full marathon, and I was doing the 13.1 mile half marathon. "Why don't you just run the full with me? You can do this. Just jump in and do it. Don't think about it," she said.

Something clicked when she said that. I took her advice. Without thinking about it, I jumped in and ran the full with her. We had a wonderful time running the race. It was nice running our first full marathon together.

After finishing the 26.2 mile race, I was officially a marathoner! I never struggled again to complete another. I went on to do a few more races of this distance, and I even finished an ultra-marathon – a 50K, 31 miles and change.

For some reason, there is often an intense fear of the unknown for us when attempting to accomplish things we have never done before. One of the best ways to overcome this is to prepare as much as you can and then jump into it. I realize this is easier said than done, but some of the ways we have already discussed in this book can certainly help, namely deep breathing and visualization.

Before doing something for the first time, steady your nerves by doing some deep breathing. (Go back to Chapter 5 if you need a review). In addition, I recommend doing some mental rehearsal a few days leading up to your event through visualization. (Go back to Chapter 6 for a review on this if you need to).

Another thing I have found helpful to combat fear when attempting to do something for the first time is to focus on the mantra: "F.E.A.R." When focusing on this mantra, decide which side of this acronym you want to be on, because it stands for two things. F.E.A.R.: "Face Everything and Rise" or "Forget Everything and Run." I implore you to face everything head-on and rise! Say this over and over to yourself until it becomes your default mode when attempting new things.

Some of us are prone to overthink; it is built into our makeup. For instance, I went through this kind of anguish when I started writing this book. Staring at a blank computer screen with thoughts racing through my head, knowing I had to fill over 200 pages with meaningful content was intimidating at first. I described the writing process to a friend as "wrestling a sumo." My publisher's advice to "just start writing" was helpful. After a few months, it started coming together, and I experienced flow. Knowing that by getting stuck in the process you can eventfully find flow will help you as well. Be cognizant of this. It is worth the struggle.

We can employ this approach and mindset in our work environments as well. When embarking upon new projects or tasks, we need to keep in our forethoughts that there is no reward without risk. I am not saying to take impulsive jumps without preparation. This could lead to career suicide.

Instead, take calculated risks when you are prepared. Strive to grow by getting outside of your comfort zone at work. Real professional growth comes to us when we are self-aware enough to know when to jump and when to stay put. The key is to not get too comfortable staying put all of the time.

I have a friend named Sanford who is one of the most educated and intelligent individuals I know. He successfully worked in corporate America for many years but did not find his work stimulating. He made the jump to another vocation and started purchasing homes and remodeling them for profit. Some think it is odd for a man with such impeccable credentials to do this kind of work, but he loves it. He likes being his own boss and working on his own timetable. In addition, he has described it to me as being liberating.

The answers are not always black and white like in Sanford's case. Maybe you are not very self-fulfilled in your job, but you need to stay put for financial or other practical reasons. Many find self-fulfillment from starting a side hustle. Start tinkering some in your free time with a different kind of work in which you find meaningful. Don't let it become a stressor. You can spend as much or little time on your side hustle as you want. Enjoy it. Monetize it, if you wish. Having a meaningful side hustle will bring more joy to your life. Plus, it will give you more energy on your full-time job, as it will give you something to look forward to on a regular basis.

A great place to get started on a side hustle is by reading Chris Guillebeau's book, *Side Hustle: From Idea to Income in 27 Days*. It is outstanding.

When faced with something you want to do but are afraid to move on, it can be helpful to ask yourself what is holding you back. If you determine that the fear of failure is the only thing holding you back, then that may be an indicator that it is time to jump and attain your desired goal. As we have discussed in previous chapters, meditation can help in building your self-awareness by streamlining your thought process.

I have heard people say before that "fear is an energy." Use this energy on your behalf. Think about the adrenaline rush you get right before you do something for the first time. Ride the wave of adrenaline when attempting something new. The best way to do this is to close your eyes before doing it and imagine how good the adrenaline is going to feel. Then do it! You don't have to be Kelly Slater riding a huge wave in the ocean off the coast of Maui or Johnny Knoxville pulling off a ridiculously dangerous stunt! You can bring this exhilaration to anything you attempt. Why not? There is nothing wrong with accomplishing a goal and feeling good at the same time.

Many of the people with whom I work overthink starting their meditation practice. They want to read about it and analyze every aspect of it before plunging into it. While I understand their curiosity, nothing beats actual meditation, so I encourage them to practice and learn about it at the same time.

Do you remember when you were a child and you experienced the joy of jumping into new things for the first time? Doing things like diving into the deep end of a swimming pool or riding your bike without training wheels for the first time brought you pure joy. Sadly, over time as adults, we can get too comfortable in our complacency to try new things that challenge us. As a result, we often stagnate and cease to grow. The next time you are hesitant to do something that you know deep down inside will make you better, take a moment and remember how brave you were as a child when facing your fears. This will propel you to go for it!

Once you are ready, don't analyze it any further; just jump into it! As Alan Watts wrote: "The only alternative to a shuddering paralysis is to leap into action regardless of the consequences."

Chapter 16
Why the Chicken Crossed the Road

"There is nothing either good or bad but thinking makes it so." — Shakespeare

In the previous chapter, we discussed how you should learn to prepare and jump into the things that matter to you instead of letting fear talk you out of them. There is a big difference between jumping into something meaningful after planning and setting a goal as opposed to jumping for the sake of jumping. When you jump like a chicken with his head cut off, you are acting foolishly and impulsively.

Let's stick with this chicken metaphor for a moment.

Whether you realize it or not, we all have a chicken. I named mine Mick. You should learn to listen to your chicken. It probably wouldn't be a bad idea to give yours a name, too.

We have all heard the old riddle, "Why did the chicken cross the road?" The typical response to this quandary is "to get to the other side." I think we need to unpack this a bit more to better understand why the chicken sometimes feels the need to cross the road.

The chicken I am referring to is our ego. Your ego is that inner-critic with the running monologue in your head. It often causes so much commotion you can't enjoy yourself. Other times it breeds self-doubt and insecurity.

Keep in mind that the ego does serve a purpose. It tries to protect us from perceived threats. In doing so, it just goes overboard and tries to control everything we do from its fight or flight perspective.

In response to our ego, we tend to do whatever it takes to escape its nagging voice. Often, we do this by trying to seek pleasure. These pleasures may come in many different forms, including, but not limited to: food, alcohol, gambling, striving for a promotion or recognition, shopping, sex, or getting approval from others.

Not all of these pursuits are bad things. However, the pleasure derived from these things or achievements is short-lived. Once the high from these short-lived pleasures wears off, we are out seeking the next pleasurable pursuit. It ends up being a perpetual cycle.

How many times in your life has your chicken ego told you that you will be fulfilled or complete if you just lose that next ten pounds? Or read that next book? Or meet your soulmate?

In trying to always seek pleasure, your ego is like a chicken trying to cross the road, merely to get to the other side. This is because we have the false illusion that the proverbial other side is always better than where we are. As we know on an intellectual level, the grass is not always greener there. The problem is that on an instinctual level, our chicken ego is constantly chatting us up, making us make move out of fear.

In his wonderful book, *Why Buddhism is True*, Robert Wright discusses how the nature of our minds render us to a constant state of "unsatisfactoriness." He says that, according to Buddhism, the human condition can be described by a Rolling Stones song, "I can't get no satisfaction." Using this as an inspiration, I named my chicken Mick Jagger.

I think the name Mick Jagger is a great moniker for my ego for several reasons. For one, Mick appears to have a huge ego himself. In addition, he struts around, similar to a chicken strutting with its feathers and always shaking its head back and forth. Like my ego, Mick seems to care a lot about what people think of him, as he is always striving to be cool. Also like my ego, Mick never tires. His energy is boundless. He never quits. Mick is relentless, still going strong, and he's over 75 years old!

Other folks have named their chickens as well. Psychologist and mindfulness teacher Elisha Goldstein calls this nagging voice "the inner asshole." Daniel Goleman, one of the forefathers of mindfulness in the West, calls his negative inner dialogue the "inner Larry David."

Whatever you decide to name your ego, have fun with it. Contrary to what we may think, the ego is not your total enemy. The least effective way to stop the incessant voice in your head is to try to block it. You will soon find out that this type of mental resistance will only make the voice stronger and louder.

Instead of trying to block it, listen and bring gentle awareness to what it is saying. If what it is saying is helpful, act on it. If not, let it go by dismissing it. Over time, practicing this approach of gentle awareness to the chicken's voice will help tame the ego quite a bit, thus the voice will bother you less often.

You can even nicely to tell your chicken ego to be quiet if what it is telling you is not helpful. If you need to, gently let your ego know that you are the boss. Every now and then, I do this by saying to Mick, "Settle down, man. Quit talking nonsense. You are overreacting. Everything is fine."

I have heard of some meditation teachers who advise their students to "have a cup of tea with their egos." This entails having a cup of tea and having a "conversation" with it, to figure out what it is nagging you about.

Another way to loosen the ego's grip is to stop labeling every experience or situation in your life as either *good* or *bad*. Instead, start getting into the practice of dealing with everything *as is*. This will do wonders for your mood, attitude, and mindset about life in general. Your chicken will be able to understand that one side of the road isn't always inherently better than the other. In doing so, it will learn to let uncomfortable feelings and emotions process through you, instead of reactively trying to run from them.

If you were to label every experience in a 24-hour period as either good or bad, you'd label most experiences "bad."

A sample list:

Waking up (instead of sleeping longer): bad

Fixing your own breakfast: bad

Having to shave and shower: bad

Driving to work: bad

Having to work: bad

A nice lunch with co-workers: good

Going back to work after lunch: bad

Receiving a text from a loved one: good

Going to the grocery after work: bad

Driving home: bad

Seeing your beloved pet dog when you return home: good

Looking at the list above, it is easy to see how we can fall into this trap in our thinking. Even if you didn't have as many bads as the person above, I am confident that your bads outnumber your goods if you think in this typical manner.

The truth is that all of the little things that make up this list also make up the majority of our lives. We spend the vast majority of our time doing ordinary, mundane activities, like picking up our clothes from the dry cleaner, shopping at the grocery store, working, or sitting at traffic lights. Despite the chicken ego's compulsion to always drive us towards pleasure, we can make our minds up to be miserable while doing these necessary tasks, or we can bring mindfulness to everything we do and enjoy the present moment. It's up to us.

Bring your full attention to what you do, no matter how mundane you consider the activity. This gets you out of the trap of having to label each and every encounter or experience as *good* or *bad*. Instead, it is *as is*. The wise Vietnamese Zen Master Thich Nhat Hanh has a saying: "When you wash the dishes, wash the dishes."

When working with college basketball teams, we often remind the players to make sure their "head and feet are in the same place." I will sometimes go up to a player who looks unfocused and say in a nice way, "Hey, man, where are your feet?" The player will look down at this feet, and I'll say, "make sure your head is in the same place." In other words, when their feet are on the basketball court, I want their minds in the same place.

Like Thich Nhat Hanh and his mindset on dishwashing, we tell the basketball players when they are playing basketball, they need to "be playing basketball." When these student-athletes are studying, their minds need to be on the books. When they are socializing, they need to be focused on having fun. It's that simple. Have your feet and mind in alignment. This is the essence of mindfulness.

Start training your mind in this fashion. When your mind wanders, get into the habit of bringing it back to the task at hand. When your mind is fully engaged in the task at hand, it is more difficult for your chicken to start speaking up.

The goal of this practice is to attain achievement, not perfection, because our minds are always going to wander. In some groundbreaking research a few years ago, Matthew Killingsworth discovered that our minds wander almost half of our waking hours, an astonishing 47 percent of the time! He also discovered that even when we are mind-wandering about things that we consider pleasant, the outcome is unhappiness. This is because when we do manage to come back to the present moment after a long session of mind-wandering, we realize that what we were daydreaming about is not real. It's brutal to realize that when we snap out of our daydream we aren't on a beautiful beach in Tahiti! Instead, we are in our cubicle at work, not fully engaged in the present moment and angry that we missed a project deadline. The key is to catch yourself and return to the present moment as soon as possible.

Some daydreaming is crucial for generating creativity, but excessive mind-wandering leads to unhappiness. There are several ways to bring yourself back to the present moment. In other words, getting your "chicken to stay in place" is not that difficult with a little bit of effort.

One way to bring your straying mind back to the present moment is to take what we call a "big belly breath." You can do it anywhere, anytime. Simply take a deep breath. Fill up your lungs with air. Inhale through the nose. Hold it for a second, then breathe out through your nose. Imagine you are breathing so much air in that you are filling up your belly like a balloon. Do this a couple of times. As you do it, concentrate on the way your belly expands and contracts while you breathe in and out of your nose. You can do it anytime, anywhere, standing or sitting. No one will even know what you are doing. There's no need to make a production out of it or bring attention to yourself. Don't breathe like Darth Vader. Just breathe! It works like a natural tranquilizer.

Having a mantra or an anchor word is another way to return to the present moment, because when left to its own devices, the mind is going to play the same loop over and over. These loops or stories typically do not serve us very well. The objective of these loops is getting the chicken to overreact to situations.

Defeat this by replacing these old, tired loops with something that will remind you to return to the present. In doing this, you will become more proactive instead of being overly reactive.

One anchor word I have employed with athletes is "BREATHE." When their negative loops start spinning and playing their self-doubting stories in their heads, they will get back to the present by simply saying "BREATHE" to themselves and then taking a deep breath. Many of the athletes with whom I work even wear BREATHE rubber wristbands in their school colors as a physical reminder to find their anchor.

I also like the mantra "Be Here Now" (from the book by Ram Dass). Anytime you find yourself slipping back into the negative thought loops that keep you stuck in the past or reaching for the future, say to yourself "Be Here Now" as a gentle reminder to get back to the present. If this phrase doesn't resonate with you, find one that does. Make it part of your daily routine.

More often than not, our chicken gets jacked up and feels the need to react impulsively and cross unnecessary roads. Often, the chicken, not being mindful, is reacting out of F.O.M.O., the fear of missing out. With a little bit of practice and patience your chicken can become calm, cool, and collected. Over time F.O.M.O. will be replaced by J.O.M.O. (the joy of missing out), because all you ever need exists inside of you. Tap into it.

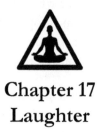

Chapter 17
Laughter

"Laughter gives us distance. It allows us to step back from an event, deal with it and then move on." — Bob Newhart

Several years ago, I was traveling to Richmond, Virginia, to give a presentation called "Digital Natives in an Accelerated Culture" for the Virginia Association of Independent Schools. I was excited to share my ideas on the need for mindfulness in educational institutions with my fellow educators.

At the time, I had been keeping consistent with a mindfulness practice of my own for a few years. As I walked towards my departing gate, I had no idea just how much my personal practice would help me on that trip.

Always early, I checked the flight information on the digital sign above the desk at the gate, and it said that we were scheduled to leave on time. I sat down to look over my presentation. I really wanted to do well and give a sensational talk, as this was one of my first big speaking gigs. I decided not to travel with a laptop, because Josh Savage, one of my faculty members who assists me with presentations, was bringing his laptop and my presentation on a jump drive after he touched it up a bit. So I pulled out a printed version of my presentation on sheets of paper I had printed off and put in a binder.

As I studied my presentation, it reminded me to give Josh a call. He was taking a later flight, and I wanted to make sure he didn't forget the jump drive. If he forgot it, we would have been screwed! Josh said he was good to go. Unlike me, he had to leave a few hours later because he had a couple of classes he was scheduled to teach that day. My flight was direct. His flight had a brief layover in Atlanta. We would rendezvous later that night in Richmond.

Or so I thought.

After studying my presentation for a while, I looked up at the flight desk. There was a gaggle of airline employees congregating. A couple were on phones and several of them were conversing with hurried, concerned looks on their faces.

I wasn't the only one to sense that something was going on, some of my fellow travelers made their way up to the desk. For 20 minutes, I watched as people were asking the airline employees what was wrong. They were told that nothing was wrong. And the more they asked, the more they were refuted. Travelers were starting to get agitated. This went on until one of the workers got on the intercom and made an announcement that our flight would be leaving an hour late due to a mechanical issue.

People started freaking out. At that point, a full-fledged scrum of angry and worried travelers swarmed the desk. Some were yelling. Some were asking questions about getting on other flights. Some were interrupting others. Some were trying to cut line. It was sheer bedlam.

Having been on delayed and canceled flights before, I was a bit concerned. I know sometimes these situations turn into a domino effect and a flight often gets delayed three or four times or gets canceled altogether. My upcoming presentation early that next morning was important to me. I obviously needed to make it to Richmond that night.

There was nothing I could do. So I sat and watched the madness unfold. I felt sorry for the workers at the desk who were taking some verbal abuse from some overly excited travelers.

After three such delays and several hours, they finally seemed to have the mechanical problem sorted out. They called us to board the plane. I was relieved that I was going to make it.

We made it off the plane in Richmond around midnight. The good news was that we were there. The bad news was that I would probably be tired for my early morning presentation. I figured that if this is the worst that happened to me on this trip, I'd be fine.

I was wrong.

I had been at the baggage carousel for at least thirty minutes waiting for my suitcase to come around. When I was the lone individual standing at there with no more bags left to claim off the carousel, I accepted the cold hard truth that my bag was lost. The reality hit me that I had no other clothes. I would be forced to make my presentation tomorrow in dirty clothes. Buying a clean shirt to replace my shirt with a food stain on it would not work, because stores were not open this time of night and they would not be open early in the morning before my presentation.

I froze for a second while I stood at the baggage carousel alone to compose myself. I closed my eyes for a few seconds, took a few deep breaths, and told myself everything would be ok. So I'd have to deliver my presentation tomorrow in a dirty shirt with very little sleep. No big deal. I could handle this. I'd rally and be fine like always.

Or so I thought.

After composing myself, I made my way to the baggage claim office to fill out a missing luggage claim. As I filled out the paperwork, the lady behind the desk was very kind and comforting. She assured me that they would find my lost bag and send it to my hotel. She said it would probably happen some time tomorrow. While I realized I would not have my bag in time for my presentation, it was at least good to know that they would return it to me at some point the next day.

Before I walked out, I explained to her that my dopp kit with my toiletries were stuck in my lost suitcase God knows where. She was kind enough to give me a Delta Airlines toiletries kit which contained a toothbrush, toothpaste, some Secret brand lady's roll-on deodorant, a cheap single track razor for shaving, and a folded up Delta Airlines t-shirt.

I thanked her and walked towards the cab stand to catch a ride to my hotel, determined to get as much sleep as I could. While sitting in the back of the cab, my cell phone rang. It was Josh. "I've got bad news, boss," he said. "My flight to Richmond was the last one out, and it has been bumped. I'm not flying out tonight. I probably won't make it to Richmond in time for the presentation."

I was almost speechless. This was now officially the trip from hell. There's no way I could give the presentation without my PowerPoint, which was on Josh's jump drive. I was screwed!

I told Josh to be careful and that I would see him tomorrow. As I closed my eyes in the back of the cab, I didn't know whether to laugh or cry. Everything that could go wrong on this trip had. Suddenly I had visions of John Candy and Steve Martin in the comedy *Plains, Trains, and Automobiles*. My journey to Richmond had been a comedic calamity just like their travels in that John Hughes classic. My trip up to this point had been a real shit show.

With this in mind, I started laughing in the back of the cab. The cab driver must have thought I was nuts, as I sat back there howling with loud, uncontrollable laughter!

I crashed hard on top of the bed like a ton of bricks when I got inside my hotel room. It was late, and I was worn out.

I woke up early to get ready for my presentation. I decided that nothing was going to get in my way. I had no PowerPoint, but I was going to wing it and knock it out of the park!

As I stood in the bathroom mirror in my dirty shirt and boxers, I went through the little Delta bag to find the cheap razor to shave. To my dismay, there was no shaving cream. I decided to improvise and lather my face with soap and use the soap as a substitute for shaving cream. This was a mistake. I nicked my chin, and it would not stop bleeding. In fact, it bled all down my shirt. My shirt now had food stains and blood all over it. I didn't have time to waste. So I jumped in the shower to get cleaned up.

When I got out of the shower, I noticed my chin was still bleeding. It apparently had no intention of stopping. I pulled off a tiny piece of toilet paper to stick to my chin, hoping that it would stop it up. It would not stop gushing out. So I left that piece of toilet paper on my face in hopes of concealing it a bit.

It suddenly dawned on me that I had no shirt to wear since my shirt was now adorned with blood spots and unsightly food stains. Having no time to waste, I remembered the Delta t-shirt in the little bag the lady gave me. It was folded up a million times into tiny little squares in the bag. The wrinkled white cotton t-shirt was not standard attire for this type of presentation, but desperate times call for drastic measures. I pulled the shirt out of the bag. The label on the tag said "One size fits all," but I don't think they had my tall 6-foot-4 frame in mind when they coined that term! The shirt barely covered me, but I had to go with it.

I must have been some kind of sight with my dirty pants, wrinkled Delta Airlines belly shirt and toilet paper stuck to my chin. I tried hard not to make eye contact with anyone in the sizeable crowd while I made my way to the mic at the front of the room. I figured making too much eye contact with them would elicit too many stares, considering my appearance.

After being introduced, I took the mic and starting explaining the reasons behind my appearance. In doing so, I retraced every minute detail of my traveling follies. As I was talking, the people in the crowd were laughing. After a while, I started guffawing as well. I couldn't help myself. The story was funny as hell! The laughter was soothing. I felt so much better seeing them all smile.

After about 15 minutes of addressing the crowd, I was interrupted mid-sentence by the back door opening. It was Josh. He was able to make it to the presentation after all. I pointed him out. As I was explaining to the crowd who Josh was and what happened to him, the entire venue erupted with laughter again. Josh held up the jump drive. "We don't need it," I told him, and I continued speaking.

I was able to incorporate the concept of mindfulness into our travel ordeals. I told them that keeping calm and having a good sense of humor in tense situations is always essential in having a mindful mindset. People smiled in agreement; it was resonating with them. We were happy and connecting.

I am happy to say that this presentation was one of my most well received ever. It was non-rehearsed and authentic. People appreciated the fact that we could use our everyday misadventures to illustrate the healing nature of having a good sense of humor. The ability to laugh at ourselves in this crazy world can serve us well. It can soothe the soul and make us feel better. Sometimes you also just have to laugh at the absurdities in life and the curve balls that are thrown your way.

Josh and I went to lunch after the presentation, recounted our adventures to each other, and laughed for another hour!

We fare better in life if we are able to laugh at things when they become ridiculous, especially silly things we can't control. By no means am I suggesting you laugh like a hapless idiot at your troubles or at others' misfortune. Take DirectTV's television commercials for example: they feature people laughing at mishaps like a soda can exploding in their faces, having the back of their seats kicked on an airplane, getting a bad haircut, or spilling coffee on themselves. Don't be this laughing hyena! There's nothing funny about this stuff.

Instead laugh at life when it becomes so ridiculous that you can't make sense out of it. In these types of situations, laughing is all you can do to keep sane. Laughter is good for the soul. Besides, like the old saying goes: "Don't take life so seriously. It's not like you're going to get out alive."

Science reveals that laughter is good for our bodies and our minds. Not only does it help relieve our stress, but laughter helps our bodies in many ways, including:

1.   Decreasing stress hormones;

2.   Increasing immune cells and infection fighting antibodies;

3.   Releasing endorphins, which makes us feel good and can even temporarily relieve pain; and

4.   Increasing blood flow at times.

While there are actual "laughing meditations," I encourage you to find the humor in life itself. Having a good sense of humor is crucial for succeeding in life with a positive attitude. Let loose and laugh a bit. You will be glad you did!

Chapter 18
Enjoy the Silence

"Remain quiet. Don't feel you have to talk all the time. Go within and you will see the loveliness behind all beauty." — Paramhansa Yogananda

As a Southerner, I am not used to this type of terrain or freezing temps, but I like it. The crisp, cool air in my face is refreshing. The last time I checked, it was about nine degrees.

All I can hear is my feet crunching the snow under me as I walk across campus. It is almost 9 p.m.. I am walking under the moonlight to my temporary living accommodations in a faculty apartment, where I have been staying the past few days, as I have been conducting mindfulness training for the students and faculty here at Deerfield Academy, a prestigious boarding school in western Massachusetts. It has a unique charm and history, one of the oldest secondary schools in the United States.

The students and faculty are in the dorms, so I have the campus to myself on this stroll. It is so quiet, I can only hear my footsteps and my own breathing. Just a few days before I arrived, a brutal winter storm called a bomb cyclone dumped over a foot of snow here. The whiteness of the snow glimmering in the moonlight adds to the serene vibe of this lovely New England setting, like a scene out of the movie *Dead Poets Society*. Walking through this campus, which was founded in 1797, is like stepping back in time. The houses and school buildings, mostly made of white clapboard, look like they came out of a Norman Rockwell painting.

The steady syncopated pace of my feet crunching through the snow sounds like a song. It makes me think of an old saying: "Music is the space between the notes." With that in mind, I believe that in some regards that life is the space between sounds. After catching myself in thought, I make a conscious effort to return my attention back to my feet.

As I continue to trek through the snow, my attention on the rhythmic sound of my feet in the snow is temporarily diverted again, this time to the chiming sound of the big clock on campus, which is letting everyone know that study hall is over.

I take a deep breath, and a warm feeling passes through me. I cherish times like this. The silence feels good, filling my soul.

Silence is undervalued in today's society. We rarely allow ourselves enough silence to recharge or to be contemplative.

One of the reasons we do not invite silence into our lives is because it is not always easy to deal with our own thoughts. Often, when we jump into our cars, what is the first thing we do? We turn the radio on. Even if there is nothing good on the radio, we would rather listen to a commercial than to just sit in silence as we drive. It is the same when we get home after a long day of work. Often the first thing we do is turn on the television, even if we have no intention of watching it! We crave background noise to filter out our thoughts.

Do your brain a favor every now and then. Cut off the static. Familiarize yourself with silence. At first, it can be uncomfortable. However, over time, you will begin to appreciate the lack of noise. In fact, it can even build up your brain power.

Findings from a research experiment in 2013 reveal that silence may be food for our brains. The journal *Brain, Structure, and Function* conducted the study using mice as its subject. The study used different types of noises and monitored the effects, and it revealed that when mice were exposed to two hours of silence per day, they developed new cells in the hippocampus area of the brain. This is the region of the brain associated with learning, emotion, and memory.

Similar studies over the years have shown that loud noise has negative effects on our stress levels, and harms our cognitive task abilities, thus negatively affecting our performance at work and school. In addition, quiet time can act to lower our stress levels and blood pressure.

I recently read a wonderful book, *Silence in the Age of Noise*, by Erling Kagge. I highly recommend it. Kagge, a Norwegian explorer, explains the intrinsic need we have to tap into silence for our own sake of happiness and sanity. In his own quest to tap into the powers of silence, he became the first person to walk across Antarctica alone, reaching the South Pole on a 50-day trek. He was so determined to get rid of noise that he intentionally left the batteries to his radio behind!

The good news is that we do not have to walk across Antarctica or join a monastery to benefit from the serenity of silence.

There may be internal sources in which to find it, like your meditation practice or your exercise routine. Some sources may be external, like art galleries or quiet parks. Even a bathtub can do the trick!

When I first started my meditation practice, the silence drove me nuts! Over time, I have come to see the silence as a refuge. I look forward to returning to it as much as I can.

There is external silence, which exists in the world around me, and there is internal silence, which I dive into in several ways.

Sometimes I take a long walk in one of my favorite places along the banks of the Mississippi River. It is so peaceful to just walk and watch the water. The silence of that scene has a meditative effect on me. It makes me feel calm and often rejuvenates my mind.

Recently, some friends introduced me to the practice of "forest bathing." This is also called Shinrin-yoku in Japan, where it was developed in the 1980s. Forest bathing, which has become a staple of Japanese preventive health care, means to simply be in a forest. There is robust research which reveals that if a person visits a quiet, natural area and walks around in a relaxed way, there are numerous calming and restorative benefits. There is a group in my hometown of Memphis that regularly meets in Overton Park's Old Forest to cultivate silence and stillness through forest bathing.

When I was a child and my parents would take my brother and me on a long car drive to reach our summer vacation destination, they would get tired of us making noise, so they would make us play "the quiet game." We hated it. In fact, we saw it as a punishment.

I now go out of my way to find what I call pockets of "silence and stillness." If I can grab a few minutes of quiet a couple of times per day in my hectic schedule, I am much more happy, productive, and easier to engage with.

For some reason, we are often uncomfortable with silence when interacting with each other. Do you ever notice that you are more comfortable with silent gaps in conversation with your old friends rather than with people you barely know?

I noticed this the other day when running with one of my good friends. I always look forward to our runs together, as it gives us a chance to catch up, as both of us have crazy, busy schedules. What I also like about our runs together is that when there is nothing to say, we both are comfortable with the silent moments. It is nice when the conversation is not forced.

Like the saying goes, "Silence is golden." Tap into it. Enjoy it.

Chapter 19
Everybody's Working for the Weekend

"Have you just watched football for the past eight hours and now you're gripped by the fear of Monday? And you've done this for 35 years and never learn." — Eddie Pepitone

It is kind of funny that Mondays have always gotten a bad rap on the radio. Songs like "Manic Monday," "I Don't Like Mondays," "Rainy Days and Mondays," and "Blue Monday" are all testaments to this. Case in point: in their song "Monday Monday," the Mamas and Papas proclaim that they "can't trust that day" and "every other day of the week is fine."

On the flip side, songs about the weekend have always glorified its perceived intrinsic greatness. There is no doubt that you have heard the rock classic staple "Working for the Weekend." The song, from Canadian rock band Loverboy, became an anthem, calling for us to grind through our work or school week so we could get to the good stuff – the weekend! Almost every FM rock station in the country would play it around 5 p.m. every Friday, quitting time, to usher in the weekend. (If you are too young or just don't remember it, do yourself a favor and look it up on YouTube. It's hard not to dig the catchy, cheesy early '80s sound of the tune and acknowledge lead singer Mike Reno's fashion forwardness with his matching leather pants, jacket and headband!)

While Loverboy's ditty about looking forward to the weekend is fun, the sentiments behind it need to be unpacked a bit. In some ways, the song represents our collective fixation with always looking forward to the next pleasurable event or moment waiting for us around the corner. However, this train of thought can be a vicious cycle of self-imposed suffering.

Are we really working the majority of our lives just to get to the weekends? If this is the case, we are wishing the majority of our lives away. When you think about it in this manner, doesn't it just seem ridiculous?

We typically spend five-sevenths of our week waiting on the arrival of weekend. In doing so, we are missing out on the majority of our lives – the present moment – because we are mentally stuck in the future, which happens to be Friday! It is almost as if our lives are on autopilot.

We make ourselves miserable by dreading Mondays. We trudge through Monday and Tuesday. Then we declare Wednesday "Hump Day," because we are halfway to the weekend. Then

Friday comes. We enjoy ourselves Friday and Saturday before getting depressed on Sunday worrying about Monday with a bad case of the "Sunday Night Blues."

Consider this: there are 62 hours between 6 p.m. Friday and 8 a.m. Monday morning. This should be plenty of time to relax, rejuvenate, and recharge from the work week. However, any benefits we receive from our weekends are often negated by ill-effects from our Sunday Night Blues suffering. As we discovered in Chapter 9, our suffering is self-induced by not accepting the reality of where we are. By wanting it to be Friday instead of accepting Sunday or Monday (or whatever the actual day of the week is), we are invoking our suffering.

Monster.com conducted a poll a few years ago, and it found that 81 percent of Americans get the Sunday Night Blues. A majority, 59 percent, said they get it really bad. Like the movie *Groundhog Day*, we relive this over and over again each week; it never ends. There has to be a better way to live.

Changing old mindsets like this is difficult, but if we cultivate new habits, we can learn how to embrace each and every day instead of falling into the self-defeating mode of "Mondays suck" and "Fridays are great." The average human life is said to be around 28,000 days. If we are fortunate to live this long, 4,000 of those days are Mondays. Are you willing to basically waste 4,000 days of your life being miserable because they are Mondays? Something tells me that on my deathbed, I would want those 4,000 days back! Imagine what happens if you add Tuesdays and Wednesdays to those days as well. The number of your wasted, miserable days jumps to 12,000!

Do you ever notice the "Irony of Monday?" I call it this because even though our collective consciousness seems to despise this particular day of the week, we often designate it as this magic day when we are going to turn our lives around for the better. Monday is always the target day of the week when we promise ourselves our diet will start or our daily exercise regimen will begin. The irony is that this magic Monday never happens, as we often get stuck in a rut and decide to wait until after the next weekend to start living the life we want. This reminds me of a funny sign in my neighborhood that hangs above a tavern proclaiming, "Free burgers and beer tomorrow." The sign hangs every day. So there is no "tomorrow."

It is helpful for us to get into the habit of seeing each and every day as an opportunity to find meaning in our lives, no matter what day of the week. We don't have to wait until Monday or New Year's Day to put goals or resolutions into action. Each experience and encounter presents us with a chance to do so. Do things that matter to you. Look at every day of the week as clean canvas, waiting for you to paint a masterpiece.

Staying active on weekends can help you break out of this trap as well. Our culture puts too much of an emphasis on the glorification of busy. I am not suggesting this. Instead, I implore you to find the happy medium between running around like a dog chasing its tail and binge watching 27 episodes of Game of Thrones. Stay active during your weekends doing things you love, being social with friends and family. This beats sitting alone in front of a television for two days, worrying about the impending start of the work week. Get off of Facebook. Unplug. Power down. Get outside.

Another way to break the "Working for the Weekend" cycle is to plan a regular Monday night activity or event. Perhaps you can find an exercise group, a trivia night, a painting class, or whatever makes you happy. This gives you something to look forward to on that day. Some folks also break up the week by having a regularly scheduled social event with friends on Wednesday nights, and instead of waiting for the weekend to see your favorite team play, why not take the family out to the ballpark on a Tuesday night?

You can get as creative as you want to with this. It's your life. Do what makes you fulfilled. Unshackle those work week mindset chains any way you want. Just remember that the only reason Mondays suck is because you think they suck, and next time you hear someone proclaim T.G.I.F., know that you can cultivate that appreciation for life on any day of the week!

Chapter 20
Pacing Fred

*"One of the secrets of life is that all that
is really worth the doing is what we
do for others." — Lewis Carroll*

A source of great pleasure for us can be when we sometimes put our own desires on the backburner to help a friend or loved one accomplish something that is important to them. Not only do we get a sense of satisfaction from helping someone we care about, but it also takes our ego off of ourselves for a while. The nagging *me, me, me* voice in our heads subsides for a bit. This is a good thing.

The article "Pacing Fred" describes one of the first times I fully realized the utter joy of putting a friend's needs before my own. It originally appeared in *The Road Runner,* the magazine for the Memphis Runners and Track Club in January 2011.

Pacing Fred

Most of my race adventures are assigned to me by my wife, Holly. She is good at finding challenging races for us in neat places. Together, we have done all kinds of events: racing a marathon in Cape Cod on the tail end of a Nor'easter, or doing a treacherous trail race up the hellish 12,000-plus-foot altitude of Leadville, or participating in a night race with 40-mph winds. She does a fine job of keeping me on my toes.

My latest outing involves one of my best friends, Fred Blackmon. He and I have worked together for almost a decade at Lausanne Collegiate School. He's a wonderful person. To know Fred is to love Fred. He has always been a positive influence and inspiration to everyone in our school community. The only fault I ever had with Fred is that he never took care of himself.

A little more than a year ago, Fred and I were going to see a movie together. Fred was uncharacteristically late in picking me up. I kept calling him. He wasn't answering the phone. I continued to call, but I could not reach him on the phone. It was not like Fred to stand someone up, and initially I was worried. After not hearing from him for a couple of days, I was furious. Over the next week, I left him a ton of messages with not-so-nice language on his voicemail. After the first dozen messages I left, I sensed something may have been wrong.

Almost a week later, I received a text from Fred. He had almost died and had been in the ICU at the hospital. He found out that he is a Type 1 diabetic. I asked him to do me a favor – please delete the voice messages without listening to them. He assured me that he never listened to the messages I left him. I hope that's true.

A few days later when I saw Fred, I was crushed by how pale and weak he looked. Once full of energy and spirit, he was moving like an old man. We had a long talk. He told me he needed to make some lifestyle changes, and he was going to hire a personal trainer. In addition, he asked me if I would serve as his running coach. He wanted me to train him, as it was his goal to complete a 5K in a few months.

I agreed to help him. I knew that training and sometimes running with someone else might detract from my own training a bit, but I was happy to help my friend. The new Fred was determined to become a healthy runner. Who was I to not support my buddy in this noble cause?

Before putting together his training plan, I looked at the MRTC race calendar to find Fred the perfect 5K for his goal race. I found just what I was looking for – a really small race close to our school. With any luck, Fred would have a great first race and possibly even place in the event. This would hook him for sure.

Over the next few months, Fred ran like a madman. He kept to the training schedule I made for him, and he worked diligently on his cross training with his personal trainer. I am happy to say that his medical reports from his physician were also outstanding. Fred was becoming a healthy man and a runner!

On the day of his first 5K, Fred was beyond nervous. I told him I would be right there with him, pacing him. I assured him he had nothing to worry about. I must say, he exceeded my expectations. He earned a third-place medal in his age group! Evidently, my plan was a success, as he proclaimed, "I want to train and run the St. Jude Half Marathon."

Over the next few months, Fred continued to train and run races of various distances. I paced him at several of these races. He would text me every night and give me feedback on his training sessions. From his feedback, I would advise him on what to do. Helping Fred also helped me with my own running. It made me think and reflect on what I was doing.

It would be an understatement to say that the week of the St. Jude Half Marathon was a pivotal period in Fred's life. A few days before the race, Fred's wife, Ellen, gave birth to a healthy baby boy, Fred Blackmon III. Ellen was nice enough to give the new daddy a few hours off to run the race.

I was delighted to be Fred's pacer for his big race. It meant a lot to both of us. Less than a year ago, Fred was on the brink of death. Now he was on his way to becoming an endurance athlete.

As we were about to cross the finish line, I looked over at Fred. His face was beaming with pride. He was a new man. I could tell by the look on his face that crossing the finish line meant the world to him. He would never be the same. I take great pride in being along for the ride during his incredible journey. I was filled with joy at my friend's accomplishment. Overcome with emotion, I fought back a tear or two. It was an honor to pace Fred. I know he would have done the same for me.

Postscript: As of 2018, Fred has now completed 29 half marathons!

Chapter 21
You Gotta Have Faith

"Prayer is when you talk to God. Meditation is when you listen to God." — Unknown

I am from the South, the so-called "Bible Belt." One of the first questions people often ask when meeting for the first time is, "Where is your church home?" Not being very religious, I always leave them with a puzzled look on their faces when I don't have an answer.

It is not that I have anything against organized religion. I think it is wonderful. It is just that I consider my spirituality a personal matter. I do have some strong spiritual beliefs, but I choose not to discuss them much with people I don't know very well. I am more about bringing people together than tearing them apart. I try hard not to have preconceived notions based on what religion or spiritual group someone belongs to. In addition, I try to let my actions speak louder than my words. In doing so, I try to emulate the words of the Dalai Lama when he says, "My religion is very simple. My religion is kindness."

When I introduce meditation to people for the first time they ask if it is a "Buddhist thing." I think some people believe that this type of practice may be un-Christian or un-Jewish, or un-Muslim. I explain to them that while it comes out of the Buddhist tradition, it does not require people to become Buddhist or adopt a certain belief system. It can be argued that Buddhism is less of a faith and more of a practice which can give us techniques for dealing with our minds. I assure them that I teach this from a secular perspective.

I have told people that meditation can be a great tool for settling your mind before you pray. There is a wise old saying that applies here: "Prayer is when you talk to God. Meditation is when you listen to God."

A while back, a good friend recommended I read *Own the Moment* by Christian pastor Carl Lentz. He knew I would like it but figured I would not read it. His reasoning behind this was because Lentz is an evangelical pastor at a megachurch, and he serves as Justin Bieber's spiritual advisor. My friend knows me well! All of that was enough to turn me off to the book.

After much prodding, I relented and read it. *Own the Moment* is written from a Christian perspective and addresses many perspectives that I would say are steeped in the concept of mindfulness. Even though I did not want to read the book initially, I ended up enjoying it thoroughly. Furthermore, I was a bit hypercritical. I always take umbrage with someone when they refuse to consider mindfulness or meditation because they think it's "Buddhist," yet I did the same thing with Lentz's book. This is like someone refusing to study algebra because it was invented by Muslims. Wouldn't that be ridiculous?

My friend Fred is a devout Christian. We enjoy finding common ground between his Christian faith and my mindfulness practice. He often sends me wonderful scripture quotes that affirm this:

Psalm 46:10: "Be still and know that I am God."

Psalm 23: "The Lord is my Shepard. He maketh me lie down in green pastures." (Commands us to be still)

Mark 4:39: "Quiet! Be still." (Jesus said to the wind.)

Exodus 14:14: "The Lord will fight for you. You only need to be still."

I believe that many Christians are possibly looking for mindfulness. This is evident by the fact that the most highlighted verses in the Kindle Bible are ones about peace and anxiety. Coming in at number one is Philippians 4:6-7: *"Do not be anxious about anything, but in everything by prayer and supplication let your requests be made known to God."*

It should be noted that all major religions practice some form of meditation. Meditation can be seen as a practice that steadies the mind and the soul for prayer. Furthermore, meditation and other meditative type of concentration techniques can help us break the stream of conscious thoughts flowing through our minds so we can focus on praying.

Examples may be found in any religion or denomination. For instance, the Episcopalians use a centering prayer for this purpose. Catholics use rosary beads to break the inundation of thoughts. People of the Jewish faith sometimes stand and sway when praying because it improves their spiritual intensity. Sanskrit mantras and Hail Marys are types of chants used to serve similar purposes. These are just a few of the numerous examples of contemplative meditative practices which may be found in any faith tradition.

Two Saturdays a month I volunteer my time to teach mindfulness and meditation in a small chapel at the Church Health Center in midtown Memphis. This beautiful chapel is housed in the enormous Crosstown Concourse building, which is a refurbished Sears warehouse and retail building. It was originally built in 1927. After sitting vacant for many years, the building was resurrected and reopened in 2017 as a mixed use vertical urban village. Our classes are free, and they draw a wide variety of people from different races, faiths, professions, and socioeconomic backgrounds. While my sessions are ecumenical in nature, I encourage participants to pray to themselves after meditating if they wish. Teaching these sessions is one of my most favorite things to do.

While I realize and respect the fact that prayer is not for everyone, research shows that there is great power in prayer. Some of the many benefits include: improved self-control, the tendency to be more forgiving, being more grateful about what you have, increased trust, and a better sense of self. It also improves attitude and outlook on life, and it gives hope.

When I was a teenager, The Police had a song called "Spirits in the Material World." The words to that song were the springboard for a bit of a spiritual catharsis for me, as they made me realize that we all have a spiritual side that needs expressing and investigating. It is important to have faith in something bigger than ourselves. Most importantly, that faith does not always come in a box.

Having a strong sense of our religious convictions works for many of us. I was always envious of those who knew what their religious and spiritual convictions were in an unwavering manner. It was never that easy for me. I have always been more of a seeker.

For those who consider themselves spiritually inclined but not religious, Timber Hawkeye has a wonderful book called, *Faithfully Religionless.* He refuses to see God as a man in the sky with a long beard who gives blessings for good behavior and condemns those who are bad. It is his contention that religion does this kind of judging, not God.

When thinking about God, I find solace from the 15th century Indian mystic poet and saint, Kabir. In his poem, *Breath,* he sees God as the "breath inside the breath."

> *Breathe*

> *Are you looking for me?*
> *I am in the next seat.*
> *My shoulder is against yours.*
> *You will not find me in stupas,*
> *not in Indian shrine rooms,*
> *not in synagogues, nor in cathedrals;*
> *not in masses, nor kirtans,*
> *not in legs winding around your own neck,*
> *nor in eating nothing but vegetables.*
> *When you really look for me, you will see me instantly.*
> *You will find me in the tiniest house of time.*
> *Kabir says: Student, tell me, what is God?*
> *He is the breath inside the breath.*

Chapter 22
Don't Worry. Be Happy.

"If you are setting out to be joyful you are not going to end up being joyful." — Desmond Tutu

As a species, human beings tend to worry a lot. In fact, most of our worry is not warranted. A recent study by Dr. Robert Leahy, an expert on the subject, revealed that 85 percent of the things we worry about never happen.

An extensive study on the subject of worry was conducted on a widespread scale in Great Britain a few years back. It revealed that the average person spends about two hours and fifteen minutes per day worrying. Over a lifespan, this adds up to six and a half years of worrying!

Even if these facts are not 100 percent accurate, it is safe to assume that we spend a ton of time engaged in needless fretting. We worry about almost everything, including our desire to always be happy.

Our collective fixation with worry and being happy was addressed in one of the biggest pop songs in the 1980s called "Don't Worry, Be Happy" by Bobby McFerrin. It became a worldwide smash and went to the No. 1 spot on the Billboard charts in 1988. This catchy piece of ear candy holds the distinction of being the first a cappella song to reach the Billboard Hot 100 Chart.

McFerrin was inspired to write the song when he was visiting some fellow musicians and saw a poster in their apartment of the Indian mystic and sage Meher Baba that read, "Don't Worry, Be Happy." This message was Baba's mantra for his followers in the West. In the 1960s it was not uncommon to see these words and Baba's likeness plastered on posters and inspirational cards.

On the surface, McFerrin's song is a fun ditty that gets stuck in your head, but on a deeper level, it gets us to question our own state of happiness and contemplate the overall meaning of just what happiness is.

Trying to define happiness in our society is no easy feat. We all have our different views on what the meaning of happiness holds for us. We hear about happiness in love songs and in the movies. Even the Declaration of Independence assures us that we all have the right to the "pursuit of happiness."

So why are we constantly vigorously pursuing something that we do not quite understand?

To some people happiness is the absence of pain and anxiety. For others happiness is comfort, while others equate happiness with pleasure.

To a certain extent, chasing happiness can be a lot like a dog chasing its own tail. It can feel futile. While we may often attain pleasure or comfort by reaching a temporary desire, the feeling often is fleeting. It only lasts long enough to leave us craving more. In essence, we fail ourselves by thinking that we can find happiness in external events, items, or experiences.

Happiness is an inside job. It starts from within ourselves. It should not be a destination unto itself. If "happiness" is your end goal, you are always going to be fraught with disappointment.

Start trying to see happiness as a state of mind instead of a final destination. Much of our suffering is caused by clinging to things and situations we cannot control. We put ourselves in a healthier state of mind if we get into the habit of not always trying to make ourselves happy. Instead, we should strive for meaningfulness in every event, situation, and interaction we experience. By looking for meaningfulness in all we do, we will often find happiness as a by-product. Don't wait. Get out and do the things you find meaningful. It will make you feel good.

As we have discussed in other chapters, your ability to stay in the present moment is the key to your happiness. For instance, shifting our mindset to accept every situation or experience as if it were served to you on a silver platter. Deal with what is given to you at any given moment, instead of wishing for another moment. By giving up the need to try and control situations in which you have no control, you are giving up much suffering. In doing so, you are more apt to find some happiness.

We need to get out of the mindset that only external things or other people make us happy. We relinquish too much control of our feelings and emotions when we do this. For instance, when someone says, "He makes me happy," or, "That movie makes me happy," they are suggesting that people or outside things have control over his or her state of happiness.

Instead, find happiness by being around people you like and by seeing movies you enjoy. See the difference? Happiness does not just happen. You make it happen by doing what you love and not worrying about whether these things make you happy or not. Being grateful will make you feel good. Having gratitude and being thankful for all you have in life will bring about feelings of happiness.

I keep a gratitude journal to cultivate these positive feelings. At the end of every day before I go to sleep, I write down at least five things I am grateful for on that day. It can be something as seemingly ordinary as a pretty sunset or something as significant as a job promotion. It does not have to be something earth-shattering every time. By making note of your gratitude on a daily basis, you are learning to look at the world through eyes of abundance instead of scarcity. You learn to find happiness in all of your experiences and relationships, instead of just seeking pleasure.

Doing things for other people will also put you in a good mood. I have found that serving others is good for my soul. It also enables me to get my mind out of my ego, where it is always me, me, me. I try to make a habit of doing nice things for people. By doing this, it is a win-win. I feel good, and they feel good as a result. We are social creatures by nature, and we are wired to help one another. What is not to like about this? We have many opportunities to do the right thing by assisting others and feeling good about it at the same time.

In one of the oldest texts ever written over 2,500 years ago, Lao Tzu tells us in Verse 44 of the *Tao Te Ching* the true secret of happiness:

> *Fame or integrity: which is more important?*
> *Wealth or happiness: which is more valuable?*
> *Success or failure: which is more destructive?*
>
> *If you look to others for fulfilment,*
> *you will never truly be fulfilled.*
> *If your happiness depends on accumulating wealth,*
> *you will never truly be happy.*
>
> *What you gain is more trouble*
> *than what you lose.*
> *Be content with what you have;*
> *rejoice in the way things are.*
>
> *If you know when to stop*
> *and realise there is nothing lacking,*
> *the whole world belongs to you.*

The world is yours. Lose yourself in a good piece of music, art, or during an activity you love. Get into the flow of what is going on. This is going to elicit feelings of joy more than anything. Sing and dance like no one is watching. If all else fails, download Bobby McFerrin's tune and heed the advice of Meher Baba. Make it your mantra. When feeling stressed and overcome by worry, repeat to yourself over and over: "Don't Worry, Be Happy."

Chapter 23
School Daze

"Education is not just about going to school to get a degree. It's about widening your knowledge and absorbing the truth about life. " — *Shakuntala Devi*

I am walking through a crowded school hallway between classes. My destination is a seventh grade social studies classroom. I am going to observe the teacher. As a principal, this is something I do a couple of times a school year. As I zigzag my way through the long hallways, I try not to bump into students. They are all over the place, frantically grabbing their books and other things out of their lockers while trying to get a quick word or two to their friends. Some are bouncing around the halls like balls inside of a pinball machine. A few are smiling. Others look dazed or more solemn. The scene is loud and busy. This is a normal snapshot on a typical school day between classes.

We do not have bells at our school. We did away with them more than a decade ago for several reasons. We figured we could squeeze more instruction time into our school day if we did away with the mandated five-minute intermission between each class period. Secondly, we didn't like the Pavlovian effect the bells had on our students. In lieu of the bells, teachers will let our students know when class is over and usher them on their way to the next class, allowing enough time for bathroom stops, water, etc. Believe it or not, it works very well.

After a few minutes, I make my way to my destination, the seventh grade classroom, and take a seat in the back. The teacher ushers the last few stragglers inside the room. Almost on cue, one of the students stands up and turns the lights off. The students sit up straight with their hands on their knees and close their eyes.

The teacher reaches for a singing bowl on her desk. She picks it up and gently strikes it with its accompanying stick. The echoing harmony from the bowl travels through the air for several seconds. The students' faces look peaceful as they focus their attention on their breathing. The teacher offers a few words of instruction, but for most of the two minutes, the children are immersed in silence. They are very still. The scene has gone from frantic to tranquil in about ten seconds.

None of the drama, worry, or stress they were dealing with in the hallway seems to be bothering them now. As they sit there with their eyes closed, I take it all in, surveying the room. Their little faces look so peaceful. I find it wonderful that we have children from various races, religions, ethnicity, and origin in this classroom, and they are all unified in this moment by what we call a "mindful moment."

After a couple of minutes, without a word, the teacher gently strikes the singing bowl to close the session. A different student gets up this time to turn the lights back on. The students slowly open their eyes. The teacher walks towards the classroom. The lesson begins.

We do this before every class at our school. Instituting a culture of mindfulness has been a positive paradigm shift for our middle school. Here is some information about it from our school website:

CULTURE OF MINDFULNESS

Mindfulness is an integral part of our Middle School community. It enhances our physical, mental, and emotional well-being.

We embody, practice, and promote mindfulness to further the social, emotional, and cognitive development of our students, and the self-care of our teachers and staff. Many of our Middle School teachers and administration have been trained in mindfulness techniques to help facilitate this objective.

Before every class period, classroom teachers lead the students in a brief "Mindful Moment" (typically somewhere between 30 seconds and two minutes long) to assist the students in getting focused and ready to learn.

In addition, our Head of Middle School teaches an optional six-week mindfulness course twice a year for students. Mindfulness trainers also come to campus several times per year to lead our teachers through mindfulness sessions to help them better deal with stress and fatigue.

Scientific research on mindfulness in schools the past decade reveal benefits for students including:

> Better focus
> Increased capacity for learning
> Improved observation skills
> Emotional development
> Increased self-compassion
> Improved grades and behavior
> Less impulsivity

We hope that your student takes full advantage of this opportunity at Lausanne, and we're thankful for your support of this program.

Implementing this culture of mindfulness has been an incremental process over the years. As I have learned with most things in life, change is more effective to all constituents involved if it is doled out over time in small doses. Years ago when I first became interested in mindfulness, I approached my headmaster, Stuart McCathie, about starting a program for our students. Being a forward-thinking British educator, Stuart gave me the autonomy necessary to do it the right way.

Initially, I had concerns about how it would be perceived by our school parents. I had read stories in the media about school systems in other parts of the country getting harsh resistance from parents who claimed that these types of programs were an attempt to brainwash their kids with Buddhism or Hinduism. I was ready for them. I did my research. Before kicking off the program, I sent them emails stating that we would be teaching this from a strictly scientific and secular perspective. I also sent links to news articles and research about how mindfulness and meditation builds up the brain, improves test scores, makes one better at problem solving, lessens impulsive behavior, and increases compassion.

To my surprise, I received no push back from parents. In retrospect, I attribute this to three factors: 1. The initial offering of sessions was optional for students. 2. We are an international school, made up of students from 55 countries. Mindfulness and meditation is a part of some of their cultures, in particular many of our Asian students. 3. Our school culture is open-minded. We are known in our area as "the school that will try anything to benefit our students." Parents know what they are in for when they enroll their children here. We have a lot of autonomy being an independent school.

When we started the program, students could opt out of recess once a week to attend the optional sessions. Despite having to miss playtime to participate, the classes had a waiting list for a few years. For three or four years, we would also bring in mindfulness teachers and trainers to train our teachers in these practices several times throughout the school year. I would do many of the trainings myself, as well.

Our program became so popular that many of the parents requested we start a program for them as well! This made sense to me, because we could teach the children mindfulness at school, but if they went home to a chaotic home life, it was all for naught. With this in mind, we started a weekly "Mindful Monday" session for parents. It was a huge hit!

After several years, I decided that optional sessions were not enough. This is why we do a "mindful moment" before every class now. From a developmental perspective, middle school children, ages 10-14, endure quite a bit of change from just about every conceivable domain: physically, mentally, and emotionally. When you reminisce fondly about your school days, I bet typically you wax nostalgic about nursery school, your senior year of high school, and your college days.

Your middle school years are likely selectively blocked from your memory bank for several reasons, namely: puberty, adolescence, and the perils of socialization. When first-time parents ask me what is wrong with their babies at this stage of maturation, I use the technical nomenclature, "It's a funky time." Their brain chemistry at this age is all over the place!

So when we consider that middle school kids are going through this "funky stage" of life and we combine it with the accelerated pace of these crazy times, a mindfulness practice for them makes sense. I believe we were one of the (if not the) first schools in the South to have such a program. Similar programs have existed for years on both coasts. I am happy to see more and more of these SEL (social and emotional learning) programs popping up in the middle part of the country, too.

I would be surprised if every school in the nation does not have a mindfulness program within the next 20 years. It just makes too much sense to not have one. It's inexpensive. More importantly, it is highly effective in teaching children emotional regulation and important coping skills in dealing with the stresses of life.

I take great satisfaction that some of the teachers at my school who were initially the most resistant toward leading the students in sessions before every class are now some of the program's strongest proponents. As one of my outstanding teachers, Robin Trusty, told me:

"As a teacher, I am constantly trying to get my middle school students focused for class and ready to learn through collaboration. Implementing mindfulness into my daily classroom routine has not only refocused my students to learn, but has also allowed me time to breathe in between classes. My overall attitude has become more poised, and snapping at my students is a thing of the past. I observe my students being more patient with one another. When we first began the practice of mindfulness, I thought to myself, 'How can this moment of breathing and reflection change the aura of my classroom?' When students and teachers are aware of the present moment, learning occurs at a higher level, emotions are put in check, and the benefits are apparent in all disciplines of education."

This kind of program works well for school children of any age, not just middle schoolers. I am more familiar with that age, because I work in a middle school. However, I have visited and consulted with many elementary schools and high schools on starting mindfulness programs in the past several years.

Children of all ages face stress and anxiety at epidemic levels due to the crazy breakneck pace in which our modern world operates. Technology and, in particular, social media have pushed our children into the "glorification of busy" mindset. In addition, they have a tough time just being. Parents sometimes, wanting what is best for their children, overextend them with too many extracurriculars and unwittingly put unrealistic expectations on them. A mindfulness program helps them to deal with their daily stressors.

A mindfulness program does not have to be anything elaborate or complex. In fact, I have seen some of the most simple ones net the best results. For instance, one time visiting a kindergarten, the teacher had the students lie on their backs. She then had them place stuffed teddy bears on their stomachs and encouraged them to watch their "breathing buddies" go up and down every time they breathed. It was magnificent in its simplicity and in its effectiveness in getting the little kids to focus on their breathing. It calmed them down and put them into a relaxed state in no time.

I asked some of our teachers to do an informal survey of our students about our mindfulness program at school. Their responses were overwhelmingly supportive of the sessions. (The following are some of their actual responses but not their real names):

> "I find mindful moment helpful both in school and sports. For class, I can gather my thoughts and set aside the thoughts from the class before, like in Spanish when I need only to concentrate on Spanish. In volleyball, the whole team takes a moment during the huddle to focus only on the game." —Terri, 8th grade

> "Whenever you do a mindfulness moment, it always helps your brain reset for the next class.

Anything that might have been getting on your mind, forget about it, and go on with your day." – Jack, 6th grade

"Mindful moments help me 'reset' after each class. They help students relax and stay focused. Mindful moments also help clear my thoughts and forget about anything outside the class that otherwise distracts me." – Mallory, 7th grade

"A student in my 8th grade Language Arts class announced to me that he had found the 5-1-7 breathing technique to be useful outside of class. He said he had a particularly difficult math problem to do but told himself to settle down and begin 5-1-7 breathing and then renewed his attempt with success." - an 8th grade teacher

"It helps me calm down a lot and makes me less stressed about the homework we might have or a big test." – Nathan, 5th grade

"It helps me calm down and concentrate on what I'm doing." – Tom, 6th grade

"It helps clear my mind about anything distracting or stressing me out and it helps me focus on the subject I am doing at the time." – Cody, 5th grade

Schools have a responsibility to teach our kids more than just the three Rs: reading, writing, and arithmetic. If you are a parent and your child's school does not have a mindfulness program, I recommend advocating for one. Another option is to establish a meditation practice with your child at home. You can make it a part of his or her daily routine. You can use the techniques in this book to help you get started. There are also plenty of resources available online. Make it fun! It will make all of the difference in the world in the life of your child.

Chapter 24
Movement

"Movement is good for the body. Stillness is good for the mind" - Sakyong Mipham

Sitting is the new smoking. We live in a fast-paced accelerated culture, but we spend more and more time sitting and looking at screens. While we as a society glorify "busy," we are becoming more increasingly sedentary. The "busy" apparently entails keeping our minds busy while sitting.

I have noticed this trend with myself. First thing when I get to work in the morning, I will sit down in front of my computer and answer emails and return texts and calls. It becomes like a time suck or a vortex if I am not careful. The next thing I know, I look up and it is almost lunch time. Where has all of the time gone? Then after a long day of sitting at work, I often go home and sit while working on my writing or presentations.

I saw one study that estimated that the average American office worker sits upwards of fifteen hours per day!

Sitting is a necessity of life. I am not suggesting you nix it from your life. We just need to make a conscious effort to try not to sit excessively.

There are a myriad of reasons why sitting too much is not good for our health, including:

Those who opt to sit more and exercise less have a better chance of developing dementia, heart disease, diabetes, stroke, high blood pressure, and high cholesterol.

The cumulative effect of too much sitting is hard to counter with exercise, even if you exercise every day.

Sitting excessively can cause deep vein thrombosis (DVT), blood clots in the legs.

There is more likelihood in becoming overweight or obese from too much sitting.

Excessive sitting and ruminating causes heightened anxiety.

Too much sitting is not good for your back or your posture.

Varicose veins may develop from sitting too much.

Our risk of cancer increases when we spend too much time sitting.

A few years ago I decided to order three or four standing desks for each of our classrooms at the school where I serve as a principal. I had no idea if they would be well received. To my astonishment, they have been quite a hit with our students. We make sure that every student in each classroom gets an opportunity to stand when he or she feels like it. The ability to move around a bit and get their blood circulating at these desks has been instrumental in helping many of them increase their focus and energy level in the classroom.

Inspired by my students, I purchased a Varidesk for the top my desk. It fits nicely on the top of my desk, and it gives me the option to stand (when I pull it up) or sit (when I snap it back down). While I am not standing the full time while at work, it gives me the option to get up on my feet and get my blood circulating a bit. There is a slight acclimation to get using to standing more. Initially, my legs were sore at first. But if you transition incrementally to this over time, your legs get used it, and it works out well.

You do not need a fancy desk to get into the habit of standing more. I have seen individuals put boxes on their desk to accomplish this. Some people find it takes time to learn how to type while standing. I understand this. If this is you, you don't need a standing desk. Just make an effort to set an alarm on your smartphone and get up and move a bit every hour.

A few weeks ago I ordered every classroom in our school a couple of wobble stools for the students to use. These unique stools gave them a chance to move around while in class. It even lets them work some of their muscles —including their core— that they would not get to work if they were sitting. Just like the standing desks, these have been a hit with the students. I plan on ordering more.

Part of the reason I am such of a fan of these stools and desks is because they promote active learning. In other ways, we are more productive and happy when we are able to unify our minds with our bodies.

Whenever I present to a team for the first time, I hope they have an old-fashioned chalkboard in their locker room. The new style white boards with the dry erase markers aren't any good. I need the old school green ones used with chalk. If I am in luck and one of these is present, I show the team the strong connection between the mind and the body by acting like I am going to put my fingernails on the chalkboard and drag them across it. Without even really doing it, some of them wince or yell. They have a physical, visceral reaction to the thought of me dragging my fingers down the chalkboard. I tell them that this is a great example of how our minds and bodies are connected! They never forget this.

I notice that when I am in better physical shape from exercising (and sitting less), my cushion time (meditation) is better. I can concentrate better and I am less distracted. It is interesting to note that the physical practice of yoga was initially used to prepare bodies for meditation prep. It makes sense.

Movement not only helps us to unify our minds and our bodies and enables us to derive physical benefits, but it also helps us grow our brain. There is more burgeoning research in the last few years about how movement and exercise primes our brain to improve our memories and our thinking skills. At the very least, exercise can be used as a mental stress reliever. An added bonus to exercise is that our bodies release chemicals called endorphins that trigger a great feeling. It's a natural high!

Much like meditation, movement can help us break out of our cluttered overthinking minds. For example if you are participating in a yoga class and concentrating on striking the next challenging pose, you are not fixated on the ruminations of your mind like: "I need to go pick up the dry cleaning and then go to the grocery. I wonder when my taxes are due. I can't stand John at work. He's a jerk." I saw a wonderful quote in the February 2018 edition of Bicycling Magazine in an article by Patrick Brady that captures the essence of a moving meditation: "Meditation is meant to awaken us, to drive our attention to the present. Nothing in my life has done this as well as the rhythmic motion of pedaling."

One of the things I like most about trail running is that it forces me to build a meta-awareness of what I am doing. In other words, I really need to be in the present moment or I will most likely trip and fall on my face! It makes me get out of my own overthinking mind. I have to concentrate on every step while running on a trail. If I miss a tree root or a rock because I am ruminating in my own head, I will fall down. This is why trail running for me is a mental and physical workout. It clears my mind, and it trains my body. Most of all, it unifies my mind and my body. In a sense, it gets me in sync.

Most schools have P.E. or gym class for their students a couple of days per week. I fought hard a decade ago to have our students have an hour of P.E. class every day. It has been a game-changer for us. I am a firm believer that working out the body is just as important as working out the mind. There are physical, psychological, emotional, and cognitive benefits to being more physically active.

If you are considering implementing more movement into your daily routine, I encourage you to start by standing a bit more and sitting less. Start integrating more movement into your life. Have fun with it. You do not have to do anything like an Ironman or a marathon (unless you want to!).

Walking is great, too. One of the highlights of the last few years for me was going on a walking meditation led by Thich Nhat Hanh. My friend and bestselling author Jon Gordon, conducts a daily "gratitude walk" in which he reflects on all he is grateful for in his life as part of this daily routine. The possibilities are endless. Do what works for you. Your mind and your body will both thank you for it.

Chapter 25
Learn What You Must, Then Keep It or Let It Go

"Some of us think holding on makes us strong, but sometimes it is letting go." — Hermann Hesse

The beauty of our minds is that they can be somewhat subjective when we want or need them to be. In other words, we can work on what we want to remember and what we want to forget. If a memory serves us well and lifts us up, we can hold on it. If a memory is painful, we can learn what lessons we need from it and then let it go.

I had a complicated relationship with my father. He was a good father, but he was an alcoholic. While he was a wonderful provider and never physically or verbally abusive, his drinking took its toll on our family.

He would get up and go to work every day, and then often come home and drink until he passed out. In today's society he would have been labeled a "functional alcoholic." Despite his penchant for the bottle, he was always loving and kind.

Eventually, his drinking caught up with his health. While I was living away working for several years in Georgia and Florida, I got reports back home from family members that the ill effects of his drinking were slowly killing him, as his drinking had increased. In fact, it was hard for me to talk to him over the phone when he called, because he was always intoxicated. It tore me up emotionally.

For the better part of a year, I was unable to talk to him. Sadly, this period of time was during the last year of his life. It was just too painful to hear his voice while he was slowly committing suicide. I could not stand it. It was out of self-preservation and for my own emotional well-being that I could not speak to him. I tried, but I just couldn't. It was tough. I loved him dearly, but I had to take care of myself.

A few weeks before he passed away, I flew to Memphis and visited him. He looked me in the eyes and said, "You haven't spoken to me in a year. You don't love me." It broke my heart. Shortly thereafter, he died. This crushed me.

For years, I had to process this. I felt so much guilt. Through much therapy, meditation, and self-introspection, I have come to the conclusion that I did what I had to do to protect myself. Despite our constant efforts, my father would never go to rehab or seek any other kind of help to treat his addiction to alcohol. You can't help someone who won't help himself.

A few years after his passing, I was on a date with a woman who asked me if I could have any wish in the world granted, what would it be? I told her to have five minutes with my father in a sober state right before he died so I could tell him that I love him. (She looked at me like I was crazy! In retrospect, I think she was probably wanting my wish to be a kiss from her. Talk about killing a moment!)

This experience taught me several important lessons. The essence of the most significant thing I was taught during this time is captured in a quote by one of my favorite authors, Ernest Hemingway, "The world breaks everyone and afterward many are strong at the broken places." The experience of seeing my father go through this was difficult, but it made me stronger in the long run. After the dust had settled, I realized that we all have things in our lives that we must endure. It is not for us to judge what others do with their lives. If we keep our eyes open, there will be a point when we realize that no one is perfect, not even our parents. We all do the best we can do on our journeys.

Having this mindset of acceptance and empathy has brought more joy to my life. It makes me more compassionate to myself and others. There is a beautiful part of Japanese culture called Kintsugi. Kintsugi is the Japanese art of fixing broken pottery cracks with special lacquer which is made of powdered gold. In doing so, this art treats the cracks or breaks as an important and beautiful part of the history of the pottery instead of trying to disguise it. I try to apply this mindset when I think of the history of my breaks, cracks, or imperfections. They have made me who I am today. They are gold.

As Pema Chodron says, "Nothing ever goes away until it teaches us what we need to know." I learned what I needed to learn from the experience with my father and let it go. Now when I think of my father, I think about the good times.

I wrote the article below for the Memphis Grizzlies' NBA website and the Germantown News in 2001. For some reason, it also appeared in a Greek travel zine. This is the way I choose to remember my dad.

> Yesterday was my father's birthday. He passed away a few years ago. Usually when his birthday comes around, it's a time for me to do some reflecting. And it's kind of strange that usually on his birthday, I think back to one of my birthdays.

> The date was May 24, 1978. It was my birthday. At the time, soccer was my life. For my birthday surprise, my father took me to the Liberty Bowl to see our hometown Memphis Rogues play the world famous New York Cosmos. Quite arguably, the Rogues were the doormat of the North American Soccer League. The Cosmos

were the class of American soccer. International stars like Pele, Franz Beckenbauer, and Carlos Alberto had played for the Cosmos. The Rogues were a rag tag assembly of rookies and washed up veterans from Great Britain.

What I witnessed that night was amazing. The Rogues were at least a four-goal underdog. In what must have been the upset of the century, the Rogues' Tony Field (a former Cosmo) scored a beautiful goal, and the Rogues held on by tooth and nail to shutout and soundly defeat the mighty Cosmos, 1–0. The screaming roar of the 10,000 or so fans at the Liberty Bowl sounded more like 50,000 to me. What a birthday gift! My father and I talked about it until the day he died. That small moment in Memphis' sports history cemented a bond between us that will last throughout my life.

In retrospect, that experience taught me that sports are a microcosm for life, and anything is possible in life with hard work and determination. If the Rogues can beat the Cosmos, anything can happen. Sports can be used to bring a father and son together.

What does this have to do with basketball, you ask? Where will you be on December 21? I hope you will be with your son or daughter at The Pyramid when the world champion Los Angeles Lakers make their first regular season visit to Memphis to play our Grizzlies. It's kind of like the Rogues versus the Cosmos or David versus Goliath. Wouldn't it be great to say that you were there when the Grizzlies upset the famous Lakers? Wouldn't it be neat to have all kinds of memories about how our native son, Lorenzen Wright, dominated Shaq in the paint? You and your son or daughter can talk about this forever. It isn't supposed to happen, but it could. Thanks, Dad. Happy birthday.

Postscript: The Grizzlies ended up defeating the mighty Los Angeles Lakers in this game! My father would have loved it.

Chapter 26
Everybody Wants to Rule the World

"In the end, the aggressors always destroy themselves, making way for others who know how to cooperate and get along." — Fritjof Capra

I am sitting in large table with 12 of my colleagues in a boardroom for our weekly administration meeting. The headmaster, our boss, asks one of our co-workers and friends a question. Having seen this before, I know what my buddy is going to do. He's going to make up some stuff that he thinks the boss wants to hear. He has no idea what he's talking about, but this doesn't stop him. He begins to pontificate. We all cringe. It's ugly. When he stops his nonsensical rant, we all laugh uncomfortably, just glad that it was not us!

I could relate to what my friend was going through. It is tough not to fall into this sometimes. For years I was the worst at not listening to people, because I was always worried about having the "right" response. In doing so, I would listen to respond, instead of actually listening to hear what someone was saying.

My friend's response that day in the boardroom seems to be the frequent norm in work settings, as I've seen it over the years quite often in different places.

With this in mind, two sentences have made me respect people at work more than anything else a person can say:

"I was wrong" and/or "I don't know."

How refreshing is it when someone has the strength and confidence to say one of those two sentences, or a variation of either? It is rare to hear this, especially in a work setting. Mistakenly, most of us are scared by this type of vulnerability. I used to think this way, but I now see this type of honesty and vulnerability for what it is: a sign of self-awareness and confidence. To be able to admit that we do not know everything and we are not perfect shows that we have a large amount of flexibility in our thinking. People respect this. We also respect ourselves more when we are patient with ourselves and do not expect perfection from ourselves and others.

Employers have begun to notice that mindfulness is a crucial skill needed for their employees, as it enhances their productivity, and it also teaches them social and emotional skills which are crucial for getting along with others and avoiding workplace burnout. Some of the biggest and most successful companies, such as Google, Apple, Target, Facebook, Twitter, eBay, Intel, Nike, LinkedIn, and General Mills, have realized this and developed robust mindfulness programs for their employees. Other organizations are starting similar programs at an astonishing rate.

Even if we love our chosen vocations, work dynamics can make us do strange things. If we are not careful, our egos can easily take over and make us overly sensitive to what our colleagues think about our work production and quality of work. It is understandable that we all want to perform good work. However, no supervisor with any semblance of intelligence is going to expect us to be perfect. If you happen to have one who is this unreasonable, find another gig!

One way in which we can relieve ourselves of an enormous amount of pressure in our respective work environments is to care less about being right in the eyes of everyone else. When you learn to master this, you will see how liberating it is! It frees us up mentally so we can perform unencumbered by our minds constantly worrying about what everyone else thinks. Who needs to waste this kind of energy? As we discussed in previous chapters, working on "thinking about your thinking" and "rewiring your brain" can help you big time in all environments, including work.

We all know that life is entirely too short to just settle for a job. We always encourage each other to "never have to work a day" by finding our calling or life purpose with a career. It would be ideal if we could all be employed with jobs that don't seem like work. However, as we know, this is usually not the way the world works. While at some point in our lives, most of us have dreamed of enacting the immortal words from Johnny Paycheck's song, "Take This Job and Shove It," most of us have practical and financial reasons why we can't do that.

It is important to try to find a vocation which is in line with your values. While taking a job for just the money can work sometimes in the short term, it barely ever works long term. In fact, this type of dynamic can become toxic for all involved.

I came to a crossroads a few years ago in my work mindset. I started getting many invitations to perform mindfulness training for teams and organizations. Invitations for speaking engagements were starting to pour in at a rapid pace, as well. At the time, I had been a school principal for close to a decade. Even though my school had always been flexible allowing me to pursue my passion of mindfulness teaching, I was getting frustrated that I could not accept every invitation due to my job duties. For a short time, I felt resentful. I even contemplated for a brief while to retire from the world of education and embark on mindfulness coaching full time.

Thank goodness I was able to step back from the situation and examine it objectively. Much of my inner turbulence with this matter was caused by my ego. The attention I was getting in the media about my mindfulness work was stroking it! My mindfulness practice equipped me with the tools to look at this whole ordeal from an objective, rational point of view. I decided that being both a principal and a mindfulness coach give me the greatest opportunity to help the largest amount of people.

There was no reason I could not do both. It's understandable to have more than one passion. I love being a principal and working with kids and serving others as mindfulness coach.

Another thing that I realized during this brief period of time was that I was responsible for causing much of my own suffering at work. As we discussed in previous chapters, suffering is often caused by being in one place and wishing to be in another place. Realizing this was huge for me. At that point, I decided when my feet were at school, my head would be at school. And when my feet were working with someone on mindfulness training, my head would be right there, working with that person on mindfulness training. We find our success at work when we strive to make each and every moment meaningful, no matter how grand or mundane the task at hand may appear.

I am delighted that I was able to make the right decision. Often when dealing with big work quandaries like this, we need to make a conscious effort to separate our emotions when making these types of decisions. Two questions I try to ask myself in these types of situations: 1. Is my ego (Mick, the chicken) trying to get me to cross the road for the right reasons? 2. Am I in a positive emotional state right now? If not, I should revisit this after calming down.

Work often elicits conflict with others because we are all trying so hard to do well and impress the "right" people. As a result, emotions can run high. People have their egos and self-worth attached to their work sometimes. Plus, we are always dealing with various personality types at work.

Because we are all made up of energy, sometimes we vibrate at different frequency levels. Some people do not have very good energy hygiene. Years ago, before I discovered mindfulness, this was me. My friend, author Jon Gordon, would have referred to me as an "energy vampire. Energy vampires wear their emotions on their sleeves. You know the type. They walk into a room and suck the energy out. My mindfulness practice has made me self-aware in not only dealing with myself, but in my interactions with others as well.

There is an individual I work with who is a nice person, but her approach and mannerisms would easily set me off. She put off a lot of nervous energy and would often interrupt me and fail to listen. My reaction to her was never nice. I could not stand being around her. We would often end up arguing. I did not even realize that my disdain for her was visible until a friend of mine at work called me on it, thus bringing this blind spot to my attention. Now that I was equipped with the knowledge of this blind spot, there was something I could do about it.

Now before I meet with this person, I take a few deep breaths in my office. In addition, I say to myself, "Get ready for some Anne moments and do not react." Preparing myself in advance in this manner has enabled me to eventually be more responsive and less reactive to Anne (not her real name!). As Frankl would probably say, I was able to put "some space between the stimulus and response." As part of my morning rituals at home before work, I include her in some of my Metta Loving Kindness practice. See Chapter 3 for a review of this. Including her in my morning Metta puts me in a more compassionate place with her. I am glad to say that we actually get along well now. In fact, I consider her a friend.

On most days around 2 p.m., I try to shut my office door and do a five-minute meditation. Not only does it work to settle my mind and emotions usually, but it also helps get me past the proverbial "afternoon sinking spell." Even if you do not have time to do a mini-meditation for five minutes during the work day, work in a few seconds every hour or so to take a few deep breaths. It will make a lot of positive difference.

Many work organizations encourage their employees to always be in the loop by expecting them to be accessible 24 hours a day though company email or texts. My first-year faculty members are usually shocked when I tell them that I do not want them answering work email after they leave the building at the end of the day. I believe that self-care is a much overlooked aspect of building a successful work culture. If my teachers are always on the clock, they have no time to decompress and recharge. When their feet are at work, I want their heads at work. When their feet are at home, I want their heads at home. Everyone benefits this way.

An effective way to slow your mind down so you can focus at work and quiet your ego is to get into the habit of mono-tasking. There is a huge misconception about our ability to multitask. When we try to do multiple things at once, we usually ended up doing a mediocre job on all of the things because our attention is spread too thin. Start getting into the habit of doing one thing at a time at work and then knocking out the next thing. It's okay to switch back and forth between tasks or projects, but trying to do them simultaneously usually ends in disaster. It's easier to toss and catch one ball at a time than to juggle six.

While not every day on the job is going to motivate us to "whistle while we work," for the most part, whatever attitude we bring to work is going to be what we get out of it when the day is done. We have a special banner in our school that reads: "WORK HARD. PLAY HARD." This is a daily reminder for both the teachers who work there and the students who work there as scholars. It has become our mantra. I am now thinking about hanging a second banner next to it that reads: "WORK HARD AND BE NICE TO PEOPLE."

Chapter 27
Our Costumes

"In most of our human relationships, we spend much of our time reassuring one another that our costumes of identity are on straight." – Ram Dass

My father was always such a good sport during my childhood. He would often take us to ball games, movies, and other events, even when it was something that he had no interest in attending himself. Growing up as a child in Memphis, Tennessee, in the late 1970s and early '80s, there were fewer events bigger than Monday Night Wrestling at the Mid-South Coliseum.

My father was more of a soccer and chess kind of guy, but he knew that we wanted to go especially badly on one particular night when our local grappling hero, Jerry "The King"

Lawler, was wrestling against outsider Harley Race for the championship belt of the world.

Back in those days, there was no Vince McMahon and national wrestling circuit on cable channels for millions of viewers. Instead, regional wrestling associations were all the rage, and Memphis was the epicenter for wrestling in the South. The storylines were less complicated and less misogynistic than they are nowadays with the WWE. Don't get me wrong. It was not high culture like the ballet or symphony, but my brother, Michael, and I went through a phase where we liked it.

Lawler, a hairy, pot-bellied local boy, was a good guy. He was known for reaching down into his tights and pulling out fireballs. Always in the nick of time before being defeated, he would throw these balls of fire into his opponent's face and end up pinning the bad guy to win the match.

Other wrestlers we liked during that time included: Bill "Superstar" Dundee from Australia, Handsome Jimmy Valiant, Tojo Yamamoto, The Mongolian Stomper, Rocky Johnson, Jacky Fargo, Tommy Rich, and KoKo B. Ware. Looking back, most of these characters were exaggerated stereotypes. These guys weren't even good actors, but this didn't deter our passion for their "sport" one bit.

What I think I liked best about Memphis wrestling back in those days was that you had good guys and bad guys. There was no in-between. To my young mind, that was a beautiful concept. No shades of gray. Everything was black or white. You loved the good guys and hated the bad guys.

On that Monday winter night, my father took me and Michael to the matches. In retrospect, we must have been begging him for a week. As usual, Michael and I had a blast at the matches. We went hoarse screaming for the good guys and booing the bad guys. The arena was filled to the brim. There were 10,000-plus rapid fans screaming, spitting, throwing things, and living vicariously through every suplex, body slam, and pile driver. Michael and I had the time of our lives while Dad sat there and read a book amongst all of the chaos and commotion.

As we were filing out after the matches were over, Dad had a surprise for us. "Hold on a second, boys," he said. "Your Uncle Lenny knows someone with the wrestling management. He has arranged for us to go back into the locker rooms and meet the wrestlers."

Michael and I were ecstatic. We could hardly contain ourselves. In the matter of mere seconds, our father went from being "the cool dad" to legend status.

A security guard was waiting on us by the gate at the end of the concourse. As he led us down the hallways to the locker rooms, my mind was running a million miles a minute. I was going to meet Jerry Lawler and Bill Dundee! My friends were going to be so jealous. I'd be the envy of every 12-year-old boy in the city of Memphis!

What I saw was not what I expected. First of all, there weren't separate locker rooms. The good guys and the bad guys shared a locker room. To make matters the good guys and the bad guys were joking around together, being friendly and sociable with one another. I was crushed.

To a somewhat lesser extent, this was similar to the time when I found out that there was no such thing as Santa Claus. Don't get me wrong. Deep down inside I knew that wrestling had to be fake, at least on an intellectual level. However, my emotional level didn't ever want to accept this fact.

We tend to like being able to put labels on people. It makes it easier for us to size them up quickly, quite often as either "good" or "bad." The lesson I internalized as a kid from the wrestlers was that it is never that easy. People typically aren't all good or all bad. We like to deal in black and white. It is much easier than dealing in shades of gray.

People are complex, not simple. We do others and ourselves a disservice when we try to size people up on first impressions. Typically, the first question we ask someone after we learn their name for the first time is, "What do you do?" Then, after we find out their occupation, we make rash judgements about their level of income, their education, and where they live. After we have that information, our mind quickly comes up with a drastic conclusion of their overall perceived value to society. All of this happens in just a few seconds. It is ridiculous!

But the madness doesn't stop there. It continues, as we often marginalize people immediately when we find out that they belong to a different political party than we do. Some individuals look down on people who do not have the spiritual beliefs that they do. In the South, some are unable to be friends if they do not support the same SEC football team! Democrats are labeled "liberals" by Republicans as if it is a dirty name. The Democrats respond by labeling the

Republicans "conservatives." Once again, you have the "good guys" and the "bad guys."

Putting labels on others is unfair. Not only is it a disservice to the ones we are labeling, but we are shortchanging ourselves of a potential opportunity to learn from someone who can teach us something we didn't know. People are multidimensional. We can't be sized up by just a handful of labels.

To see an example of how we label people, think about your high school days. There was the popular crowd, the jock crowd, the geek and nerd crowd, the stoner crowd, etc. Once we were assigned to one of the labels, it was virtually impossible to shed that label and move to another crowd. The John Hughes classic '80s movie The Breakfast Club illustrated this magnificently with Molly Ringwald as the popular girl, Emilio Estevez as the jock, Michael Anthony Hall as the nerd, Judd Nelson as the stoner, and Ally Sheedy as the weirdo.

Labeling ourselves is just as detrimental. When we label ourselves, we end up "putting on costumes" and playing roles instead of being our authentic selves. I have done it to myself many times. When I get into my "school principal mode," I feel like I have to act, think, or speak the way a principal does. It puts me in a box. Sometimes when I teach mindfulness, I fall into the same trap – I feel I have to act the way that a mindfulness teacher is expected to act, whatever that is!

Ram Dass has an insightful quote about this type of behavior: "In most of our human relationships, we spend much of our time reassuring one another that our costumes of identity are on straight." While there are social norms and conventions we should follow at times, walking too narrow a path based on our self-imposed labels is limiting. I make a conscious effort to try to break out of this train of thought when I fall into it.

Whenever I work with basketball teams, I ask the players to tell me who they are. Often some will respond with, "I'm a basketball player." I will quickly correct them with, "You are a guy who plays basketball." See the difference? If he is simply a basketball player, his self-worth will be dependent on how he performs each game. It is healthier to be a "guy who plays basketball." This way he is still authentic to who he is, no matter how well he played the night before. His self-worth is not conditional this way.

I have a good friend who was a very successful triathlete. She lived for training and racing. In fact, she was very myopic about it. It seemed that every time she spoke, it was about triathlons. A few years ago, she found out that she could not race anymore due to a health condition. It threw her for a major flip, because basically her entire identity was wrapped around her racing. By playing this role and only this role, she was limiting herself. It took her several painful, agonizing years to shed this "costume."

A few years back I became a vegetarian. I must confess, I am not a very good one! When I made the decision to embark upon this, I made the mistake of labeling myself one to everyone I knew. Now all of my friends give me a hard time when I slide and eat meat. My friend Drew was smarter than me with this. He avoided labeling himself a vegetarian when he decided to go meatless. When people ask, he simply says, "I just try to eat clean." He gets no grief from our friends when he slides!

I received even more self-induced grief years ago when I started my meditation practice. I was so excited that I went around and told anyone that would listen that I am a "meditator." The grief and ribbing I got from my friends and co-workers was relentless! Every time I walked in to the room I would be greeted with "OMMMMMMMMM." In retrospect, it was funny. However, I have learned that it is better not to fall into the trap of labeling yourself. By doing so, you almost become one dimensional to others.

Our costumes are not solely limited to the micro level, as society has cultural norms that often force us to wear costumes – or in this case, masks – as well. A prime example of this is illustrated in the outstanding documentary film *The Mask You Wear* by Jennifer Siebel Newsom. This film shows how American boys are constantly pressured to "be a man" and disconnect from their emotions. This extremely limited view of masculinity causes all sorts of issues for boys in our society, as they are taught that vulnerability is a weakness or character flaw. As a result, our boys often grow up becoming confused, angry, and inauthentic men. Inspired by the film, author Lewis Howes penned a book called *The Mask of Masculinity* in which he reveals the nine masks that men wear and ways to work on taking them off. If you're interested in this subject, both the film and book are well worth your time.

Females have unique pressures to adorn costumes and masks in our over-sexualized society. At a young age, girls become bombarded with images and messages from Madison Avenue, social media, and pop culture on what it takes to be a woman. Sadly, most of these messages are telling them that being popular and sexy is everything. As a result, girls often resort to "dumbing it down" at school because society teaches them that females should be pretty, not intelligent. Young females can learn to see through this illusion by having real-life quality role models and mentors.

To snap out of this type of labeling, role-playing, and mask-wearing, we must ask ourselves a series of questions from time to time: 1. What role am I trying too hard to play? 2. Am I worried about someone seeing me without my costume on? 3. Am I labeling myself? 4. Am I labeling others and sizing them up quickly instead of getting to really know them?

Another effective way to get to know your authentic self is through meditation. Over time your meditation practice will help you recognize the voice of your ego which is constantly grasping to put on costumes in order to play roles. You will learn to listen to the voice and see it for what it is, nonsense.

Gratitude techniques, such as the Metta Loving Kindness Practice from Chapter 3, will help break you from the habit of labeling others. This practice will transform your relationship with others and the world in general.

When you strive to be your authentic self, you begin to notice the rich, beautiful uniqueness in others. You start to see that people are not always what they appear to be. Being yourself lets you break free from the corrosion of conformity. According to Nietzsche, "The individual has always had to struggle to keep from being overwhelmed by the tribe. If you try it, you will be lonely often, and sometimes frightened. But no price is too high to pay for the privilege of owning yourself."

Chapter 28
Pets

"I have lived with several Zen masters –
all of them cats." — Eckhart Tolle

I have often thought about traveling to India to find a teacher. How cool would it be to have your own personal Zen master to teach you about mindful living and being in the moment?

My wife says, "We have two spiritual masters right here: Artie and Winnie (our dogs); we don't need to go anywhere."

I initially laughed at her response, but after thinking about it, I saw she was right. We had two Zen masters living under our roof. I don't know how I missed it before.

Artie and Winnie are both distinctly unique in their own ways. Artie is a three-year-old black lab. Many people are intimidated by his big size, as he weighs over 100 pounds, but he is a big baby. His pastimes include cuddling and eating.

Winnie, our 10-year-old white standard poodle, on the other hand, has a fiercely independent personality. She is loving but likes to do her own thing. We don't dare have her groomed with the typical poodle cut. She prefers have her springy white hair grown out like a white Rastafarian. We love them dearly and spoil them rotten. I never understand when people say that dogs don't have souls. Meeting these two and getting to know their distinct personalities would dispel that myth for anyone.

I have heard individuals say before that dogs do indeed have souls because they are bodhisattvas, enlightened beings in the Buddhist tradition – they are motivated by tremendous compassion for the benefit of all sentient beings.

No matter what your stance is on whether our pets have souls are not, one thing cannot be debated: our dogs and cats embody the concept of mindfulness. As Eckhart Tolle said, "It's so wonderful to watch an animal, because an animal has no opinion about itself. It is." They are full of love and unconditional compassion. No matter what kind of day I have had at work, when I come home and walk through the door at the end of the day, Artie and Winnie meet me like adoring fans greeting a rock star. They are always happy to see me. I could be the most miserable son of a bitch in the world, but they don't care.

If we look hard enough, there are a bunch of lessons we can learn about living mindfully by observing our beloved pet dogs and cats, including:

> They live fully in the present moment and are not concerned with the past or future.
>
> They don't multitask. They do one thing at a time.
>
> They are often content with just being.
>
> They give their full presence when they are with you.
>
> Cats eat in a slow, mindful manner.

Dogs show great compassion to those around them most of the time (Cats do it when they want to!).

They focus on self-care.

They do not hold grudges (at least not for long).

They have awareness for others.

They are happy and eager to greet each day.

They realize the importance of play.

They approach things in a curious manner.

The list above is just a small sample of the many ways in which our pets serve as our everyday Zen masters. Not only do they model mindfulness for us with their actions, but they also afford us opportunities to have mindful moments in our interactions with them. A great way to break the unconscious stream of thoughts and mental clutter in our heads is to just sit with our pets and love on them. Simply petting your dog and cat on the head will do this. It's amazing how it will clear your mind and melt away worries. Try it for a few minutes the next time you are uptight. It's a win-win for both you and your pet!

The school where I work has a pet therapy dog in our Upper School division. Her name is Willow. Whenever the high school students are stressed, they can come into the counselor's office and play with or pet Willow. They absolutely love it, and so does Willow! Willow is always popular, but she is especially busy during exam season when the kids are really stressed out.

Pets are wonderful for small children as well. They teach them compassion, unconditional love, and responsibility. Pets are also great for the elderly, who might otherwise be alone.

Our next door neighbor has a dog named Radar. Winnie either hates him or is deeply in love with him, because whenever they are both outside, she barks madly at him. It used to bother me whenever I was inside trying to meditate. Now, instead of letting it aggravate or distract me, I use the sound of her bark as a "mindfulness bell." A mindfulness bell is anything that reminds us to turn our attention back to the present moment.

Chapter 29
Ch-Ch-Ch-Ch-Changes

"It all goes away. Eventually, everything goes away." — Elizabeth Gilbert

As I wake up this morning and make my way to the bathroom, my body is stiff. My knees crack and pop. My back is a bit tight. It has been this way the last few years, probably since my mid-40s. Eventually, my body will warm up and feel better, but early mornings are always a bit rough. As I look at myself in the mirror, I notice that I have a few more lines on my face and my hair is turning a bit gray and starting to recede. These are observations, not fixations for me. I realize that the alternative to getting older is not getting older. I'll take it.

Everything changes. In fact, change is the one constant in life. Nothing remains the same, and nothing remains forever. The Buddhist tradition embraces the concept of impermanence, the belief that nothing in the world is fixed or permanent. Decay is a fact of life. Existence is always in a state of flux.

As I continue to look in the bathroom mirror at myself, I think about how not all the changes I have undergone over the years are physical. Science has told us for years that every cell in our bodies is replaced with a new cell about every seven years. Whether this is true or not, I do know that I'm not the same man I was at 20 or 30 or even 40. I have changed physically, mentally, and emotionally over the years. The process of life is fluid. At every stop along the way, my priorities and values have changed or at least shifted a bit from time to time.

Staring at my reflection, contemplating the life I have lived and the life I still have to live, David Bowie's song "Changes" comes to mind. I hear him singing in my mind, "CH-CH-CH-CH-CHANGES." The song is a reflection on the passage of time and the impermanence of our existence and life itself.

I want to think that I have become a better person over time, having learned from my mistakes and matured along the way. For this reason, I have great respect for Asian cultures that hold their elders in high regard. This runs counter to our youth-obsessed culture in the West. We crave to stay young at all costs. This ends up hurting our collective consciousness.

Much of our suffering is self-inflicted. Suffering is the result of our clinging to or craving impermanent things, desiring for them to be permanent. A good example of this is life itself. Instead of living fully engaged in each and every present moment, we spend a lot of time worrying about our eventual deaths, and get attached to the hope of an eternal afterlife.

Life is what happens between birth and death. This is true for all of us. The one way to have a magnificent meaningful life is to realize this and enjoy each and every moment.

Eckhart Tolle sees life as an opportunity to strip away our costumes and masks. His philosophy sees death as a chance to strip away all that is not you, to "die before you die."

There is great liberation in fully internalizing two things on a deep level: 1. I will die one day. 2. Every day I live is an opportunity to create something special in my life journey. Alan Watts encapsulated this in his quote, "We have been taught that the going away of life is against life, but as a matter of fact, life is entirely something that always goes away. Going away – dissolving – is the same thing as living. But if we are taught that dying is against life, then we can't live."

Our lives are pretty much divided up into thirds. We spend one-third of our lives sleeping (eight hours per day), one-third of our lives working (another eight hours per day), and the remaining one-third (eight hours per day) doing whatever we want or need to do – commuting, cleaning, home and family responsibilities, etc. How much of our time during our lives is actually spent engaging in the F word? The F word is fun!

As cliché as it sounds, we owe it to ourselves to have as much fun as possible during our short time on the Earth. Very few people on their deathbeds say something like, "I wish I could have spent just a few more hours working at the office." Or, "I wish I could have spent a lot more time worrying and obsessing about shit that never actually happened." Instead, they think about the good times with family, friends, and loved ones.

Life in our accelerated culture can be insane. Many of us spend our whole lives working and slaving to the grind, thinking about the future. We dream about how happy we will be when we can retire and do whatever we want. The Dalai Lama sees right through this madness. At an event a few years ago, he opined to the Western media on what the biggest issue in the world is, he said, "Man. Because he sacrifices his health in order to make money. Then he sacrifices money to recuperate his health. And then he is so anxious about the future that he does not enjoy the present; the result being that he does not live in the present or the future; he lives as if he is never going to die, and then dies having never really lived."

The future is not guaranteed. To fully live a mindful life, we must try to live in the present moment. It is good to plan for the future, but not to obsess about it every waking moment. The best way to plan for it is to take care of the present moment and each and every opportunity as it presents itself. By doing this, the future will fall into place.

While to our Western minds a picture or image of a human skull may represent death, to some Eastern cultures, skulls are used to remind us to embrace the belief that we must transcend both life and death. In a sense, images of skulls serve as a reminder that life is short, and we should make the most of it.

We don't need to carry around a skull like they did in Shakespeare's Hamlet as a reminder of our eventual demise, but it's not a bad idea to remind ourselves that the clock is always ticking. As punk rock legend and spoken word artist Henry Rollins says, "No such thing as spare time, no such thing as free time. All you got is life time. Go."

Chapter 30
Remembering to Be Mindful

"We are what we repeatedly do. Excellence, then, is not an act, but a habit." — Will Durant

Now that you are at the end of this book, it is my hope that you will take some of these practices and ideas that have resonated with you and start your own mindfulness practice or integrate them into your existing practice. The concept of mindfulness is simple. The difficult part of it can be sticking to your practice consistently. Our goal is growth, not perfection.

Remember to see your practice as a radical form of self-care. Some people mistakenly see mindfulness as self-indulgent or selfish. This is ridiculous. In fact, you are better to other people when you take care of yourself first.

Here are some tips to help you remember to be mindful:

> Post a note on your bathroom mirror. This way you will see it first thing every morning.

> Set "mindful moment" reminders on your smartphone. There are also apps you can get to randomly ring a mindful bell throughout the day.

Have a mindfulness buddy or a group to hold you accountable. This can be a group who meets regularly in person or it may be a mindfulness or meditation online support group or forum.

Have a regular standing "mindfulness date" with yourself. This is your time. It can be the same time every day. You can also have a weekly "mini-sabbatical" date for a few hours. This can be for longer guided meditations, mindful walking, pockets of silence, etc.

Practice cooking and eating mindfully.

Take a bath or shower before bed. Use it to practice mindful bathing.

Have a designated space in your home just for meditation. Consider creating an altar with your favorite mindfulness/meditation images or artifacts. Get creative with it. Have fun.

Meditate when you wake up every day. Use an app to keep track of your consecutive days. Daily consistency is more important than the amount of time in each session.

Use some guided meditations. Mix it up with your regular meditation routine. Keep it fresh.

Read books on mindfulness.

Wear a physical reminder to remind you to mediate and to be mindful. A mala (meditation bracelet) is a nice anchor. We use rubber "BREATHE" bracelets for the teams I work with.

Remember how good you feel after you meditate.

Make everything you do a "meditation" by always trying to bring meaning to the present moment.

Make brushing your teeth a mini-meditation. When your mind starts to wander, bring it back to the physical sensations, the taste of the toothpaste, the smells, etc.

Change your posture when sitting from time to time. Straighten your back.

Remind yourself to take a deep breath and focus on the present moment every time you enter or leave a room.

Practice going to bed with an attitude of gratitude, being thankful for all you experienced during the day.

Find meditation and mindfulness podcasts you like and subscribe to them.

Follow mindfulness and meditation teachers or groups you like on social media.

Have fun with your practice! You are more likely to stick with it if you look forward to it every day.

• • •

Acknowledgments and Gratitude

First and foremost, I would like to thank my wife, Holly. She is my rock. Without her love and encouragement of all of my endeavors, I would not get very much done. I am eternally grateful and lucky to have her as my best friend and better half. She continues to inspire me every day though her words and actions.

My mother, Natalie, has always been my biggest fan and supporter. Her unconditional love and support have always been unwavering. The feelings are mutual. I appreciate all she has done for me, which is a lot.

I have had the pleasure of working with all of Will Wade's teams over the years: Chattanooga, VCU, and LSU. He is a loyal friend, my running partner, and a confidant. Thank you, Will, for all you have done for me. You are the best.

The three seasons I worked with the players on the University of Memphis basketball team started this whole ball rolling. I loved every minute of it. Thank you, Josh Pastner, for being kind enough to give me my start in mindfulness coaching. You will always have a supporter and friend in me.

Two of my favorite authors, Jon Gordon and Timber Hawkeye, were quite helpful to me in this process. Jon is a great dude who "walks the walk!" He was never too busy to take my call or text. Thank you, friend! Timber is the publisher of this book. His book, Buddhist Boot Camp, was a huge inspiration to me. I am grateful that Timber agreed to show up to my mindfulness class on short notice when he was visiting Memphis. It is an honor to now call him a friend.

Cody Worsham, the editor of Tiger Rag Magazine, The Bible of LSU sports, is the editor for this book. Thank you for letting me use your feature article about me as the first chapter of this book. I also appreciate the hospitality you always show me in Baton Rouge. Geaux Tigers, buddy!

I have worked at Lausanne Collegiate School for many years. It is a wonderful place. I appreciate that whole community, in particular Stuart McCathie, for his support, mentorship over the years, and for letting me pursue my professional passions. I am also eternally grateful to my long-time assistant principal, Kim Thorpe, and administrative assistant, Liz Kirschner, for tolerating me over the years.

I am eternally grateful to Sedale Scullark for the honor of serving as his mentor. I do not have a son, but if I did, I would hope he would be a lot like Sedale. I am proud of you.

Thank you, Coach Jamion Christian and Mount St. Mary's University Basketball for the continued support and friendship over the years. You guys rock.

Last but certainly not least, I would like to honor everyone who has ever taught me and everyone who has ever let me teach them. The privilege has been mine.

About the Author

Greg Graber, a long-time educator, teaches mindfulness and meditation to sports teams, schools, and various organizations around the world. He has worked with top sports teams like the *NBA's Memphis Grizzlies*, *LSU*, *VCU*, the *University of Memphis*, and *Mount Saint Mary's University*. He's been contracted by organizations like the *Hilton Worldwide Hotels*, *Shamrock Foods*, and the *Virginia Department of Corrections*.

Greg's work has been featured in the *New York Times* and on *ESPN*, and he has presented at *Harvard University Graduate School of Education*.

As the Head of Middle School at *Lausanne Collegiate School* in Memphis, Tennessee, Greg has developed the Unplugged Mindfulness Program for students and teachers, and he consults with other schools on developing similar mindfulness programs. He often speaks at conferences, and may be contacted through his website at **GregGraber.com**

Notes

_____

_____

_____

_____

_____

_____

_____

_____

_____

_____

_____

CPSIA information can be obtained
at www.ICGtesting.com
Printed in the USA
FSHW02n1940070818
51249FS